PRAISE FOR THE BOOK

'Simple, direct, and soulful, Vishwas's journey captures hearts and depicts the endless possibilities of the human spirit.'

– Vivek Shanbhag, novelist

'This paradigm-shifting series forces one to reexamine their beliefs. Vishwas's resolve and patience are immensely inspiring and a testament to the enduring power of resilience shown in the face of adversity.'

– Samhita Arni, author

'The stunning visuals and poignant prose combine to create a story of perseverance and valour that will resonate with readers of all ages.'

– Doug Roland, Academy Award-nominated social impact filmmaker

'This inspiring narrative brought alive by moving illustration is vital in understanding empathy and can be enjoyed across age groups. Over time, the series will find a special place among graphic novel readers in India.'

– Sanjoy Roy, co-founder and managing director of Teamwork Arts

'*Grit: The Vishwas Story* is a motivational adventure with images that take you on an inspiring, visual journey. There is so much to learn from the incredible lessons of resolve and persistence speckled throughout the story.'

– Marco Santini, global artist and educator

'The road to discovery of our true self – to me, that's the real story of *Grit: The Vishwas Story*. Do the rest of us succumb to the conditions of life and its elements, or do we tell ourselves that there is so much more to be overcome? Vishwas tells me, there are many lives to live in this lifetime.'

– Joi Barua, singer and music composer

Also in this series by V.R. Ferose and Sriram Jagannathan

'Major DP Singh is an inspiration and *Grit* has captured his journey beautifully. A must read for all ages.'

– Dr Kiran Bedi

hachette INDIA

GRIT

THE VISHWAS STORY

VISHWAS KS

VR FEROSE

SRIRAM JAGANNATHAN

First published in 2022 by Hachette India
(Registered name: Hachette Book Publishing India Pvt. Ltd)
An Hachette UK company
www.hachetteindia.com

1

Inspiration: Vishwas K.S.
Vision and concept: V.R. Ferose
Design, script, art: Sriram Jagannathan

Paperback edition ISBN 978-93-93701-45-9
Hardback edition ISBN 978-93-93701-44-2
Ebook edition ISBN 978-93-93701-46-6

Hachette Book Publishing India Pvt. Ltd
4th & 5th Floors, Corporate Centre,
Plot No. 94, Sector 44, Gurugram – 122003, India

Prelims typeset by Manmohan Kumar

Printed and bound in India
by Manipal Technologies Limited, Manipal

VISHWAS K.S.

To my dear wife, Lakshmi, who keeps me anchored with her love and friendship. To my beautiful daughter, Prashasti K.V., the apple of my eye and the perfect addition to our little family. My mother, Usha M.S., my father, Sathyanarayanamurthy K.V., and my grandmother, Shakunthalamma, for their unconditional love and countless sacrifices. I'd also like to thank Astha Foundation, the Vijayanagara Aquatic Centre, the *Arabbie* team, and the rest of my family, friends, mentors, well-wishers, trainers, dance choreographers, and swimming coaches for their time, care, and generosity over the years.

V.R. FEROSE

To Vivaan, for being the inspiration and the trigger for the inclusion movement. To Deepali, the unsung hero, the silent warrior and the love of my life. To family, friends and all the volunteers in the inclusion movement.

SRIRAM JAGANNATHAN

To Amma, Appa – thank you for everything. And, happy 50th anniversary!

FOREWORD

Nothing stirs hope in us more than stories of those who have survived against all odds. It is human nature to seek inspiration in others who have forged their path to success. It's not money or rank or material comfort that illuminates our own journeys, as many believe and thoughtlessly chase, but the patience to endure stressful and difficult times, and the grit to fight against impossible odds. It is to measure the quality of life by the relationships one has built and sustained, the grace and resolve one has shown in the face of misfortune. No one portrays these values more than Vishwas. When he was ten, he lost his arms and his beloved father in a tragic accident and bravely chose to ride the turbulent waves rather than drown in them. He threw himself into a wide range of activities, testing his body's limits. It turns out that there were none. What an abled, privileged person could do, Vishwas did better. His achievements have a lot to do with his talent, surely. But his determination to not be the victim of his circumstances, but rather the hero of his story, led him to where he is today – a successful para-swimmer, dancer, martial artist, and the alchemist of turning tragedy into triumph. It's no ordinary feat.

Written and illustrated by Sriram Jagannathan, this graphic novel perfectly balances an economy of words with stunning, impactful illustrations. Sriram has sensitively narrated the events of Vishwas's life, giving him strong agency in this engaging, fast-paced biography. Reading it is like watching a movie on paper. The Grit series by V.R. Ferose and Sriram Jagannathan, chronicling the tales of exceptional achievers, is a memorable read and an essential addition to school libraries to inspire young minds to reach for the stars despite the challenges life throws at them. Stories like these pave the way for a more inclusive, compassionate and informed society in today's increasingly riven world.

I wish Vishwas more glory, and salute his courage and unwavering determination.

Ramesh Aravind
Actor and director

ACKNOWLEDGEMENTS

First and foremost, we would like to thank Abhivyakti Singh, our thoughtful editor, for making this graphic novel the best version of itself. Priya Singh, Vice President – Product & Digital Resources, for her invaluable expertise throughout the journey. Our deep gratitude to Parul Sharma and Ashutosh Sharma for their keen eye, and Thomas Abraham, MD, Hachette India, for his friendship and support in bringing this series to fruition. And last but not least, the rest of Team Hachette across departments without whom this publication would not be possible.

PREFACE

Life can be difficult, and a key measure is a person's ability to overcome adversity. And not many withstand or overcome hardships with as much grace as Vishwas. I first met him in Bengaluru for the India Inclusion Summit (IIS) 2019 on a pleasant November afternoon. He had performed on stage to roaring applause after the release of the IIS theme song, which he was a part of. It was impossible not to be captivated by his simplicity and, above all, his contagious optimism and independence. After exchanging pleasantries, he typed on his phone with his feet to store my number. A friendship began.

Since then, every conversation with Vishwas has taught me something about myself and the world in a broader, more compassionate context. One does not meet someone like him often – earnest, extraordinarily resilient and unaffected by the travails of life. His sense of gratitude is almost baffling. But such is Vishwas – focused on the bigger picture, humble to a fault and generous without any caveats.

In March 2020, when COVID-19 took over the world, his income experienced a devastating hit. Invitations to events and TV shows declined overnight. He couldn't maintain his swimming practice sessions because the pools had shut down. The biopic that he had just begun shooting came to a screeching halt. The only source of income keeping him afloat was the twelve thousand rupees he received as rent, a meagre sum he had to budget and stretch to bring up his infant daughter. For a man who has built his life from the ground up many times over, distress was not new, but it was heartbreaking all the same. But Vishwas never complained. He stayed hopeful for a better and brighter future.

Light has begun to seep back into his world. Vishwas has since then completed the shoot for his biopic, *Arabbie*, which is now ready for release. Due to long delays and substantial budget overruns, the movie has yet to find a theatre or OTT release. But he is patient. He understands his life has never been easy – everything he has achieved has been despite obstacles and challenges. So, with a firm resolve and unmatched grit, he continues to forge ahead.

A life story as captivating as the man himself, this is *Grit: The Vishwas Story*.

V.R. Ferose

1

I'M VISHWAS.
I'M A SWIMMER.

THE REACTION TO THIS INTRODUCTION HAS BEEN MORE OR LESS CONSISTENT OVER THE YEARS.

THAT'S WHEN MY FRIENDS COME TO MY RESCUE.

speedo
CAN AM PARA-SWIMMING CHAMPIONSHIPS
July 15-17, 2016
Name : Vishwas Kalahasthipur Sathyanarayanamurthy
Team India
Swimmer
SB6
AND, THIS. THIS WAS IN CANADA.
WOW, THIS IS MIND-BLOWING!
ISN'T IT?
SEE, THAT'S OUR VISHWAS!
THIS INTERNATIONAL MEDAL MUST HAVE BEEN THE PINNACLE OF YOUR CAREER!
YES, IT WAS.
AND THERE HAVE BEEN OTHERS, TOO.

IDM BERLIN 2017
YOU MEAN, THIS ONE IN GERMANY?
MMM, YES. THAT AS WELL.
THIS IS SO AMAZING!
MY GOD, SO MANY MEDALS!
WHICH ONE'S YOUR FAVOURITE?
OH, I DON'T KNOW. EACH ONE IS SPECIAL.
OH, COME ON! YOU MUST HAVE SOMETHING, SURELY. THE WIN THAT YOU ENJOYED THE MOST, OR AN EVENT...

MMM...
...IF I HAVE TO PICK ONE...
...I THINK IT HAS TO BE MY VERY FIRST COMPETITION...
...IN MADHYA PRADESH. THAT WAS IN 2014.
AH, OF COURSE. THE FIRST IS ALWAYS THE BEST!
I REMEMBER MY FIRST SCUBA DIVE. SO THRILLING!
YOUR FIRST MEDAL, AND THAT TOO IN YOUR FIRST COMPETITION! THAT WOULD'VE BEEN-
OH, NO NO. I DIDN'T WIN ANY MEDALS THERE.
OH!
BUT THAT WAS A GREAT LEARNING EXPERIENCE FOR ME.

IT WAS A NATIONAL COMPETITION...
NATIONAL PARA-SWIMMING
COMPETITION - 2014
BHOPAL
...ATTRACTING SWIMMERS FROM ALL OVER THE COUNTRY.
MANY WERE SEASONED ATHLETES.
SO, NATURALLY, I WAS VERY NERVOUS.
TAMILNADU

BUT SOMEHOW, I FELT AT EASE WHEN I WATCHED THE FIRST RACE.

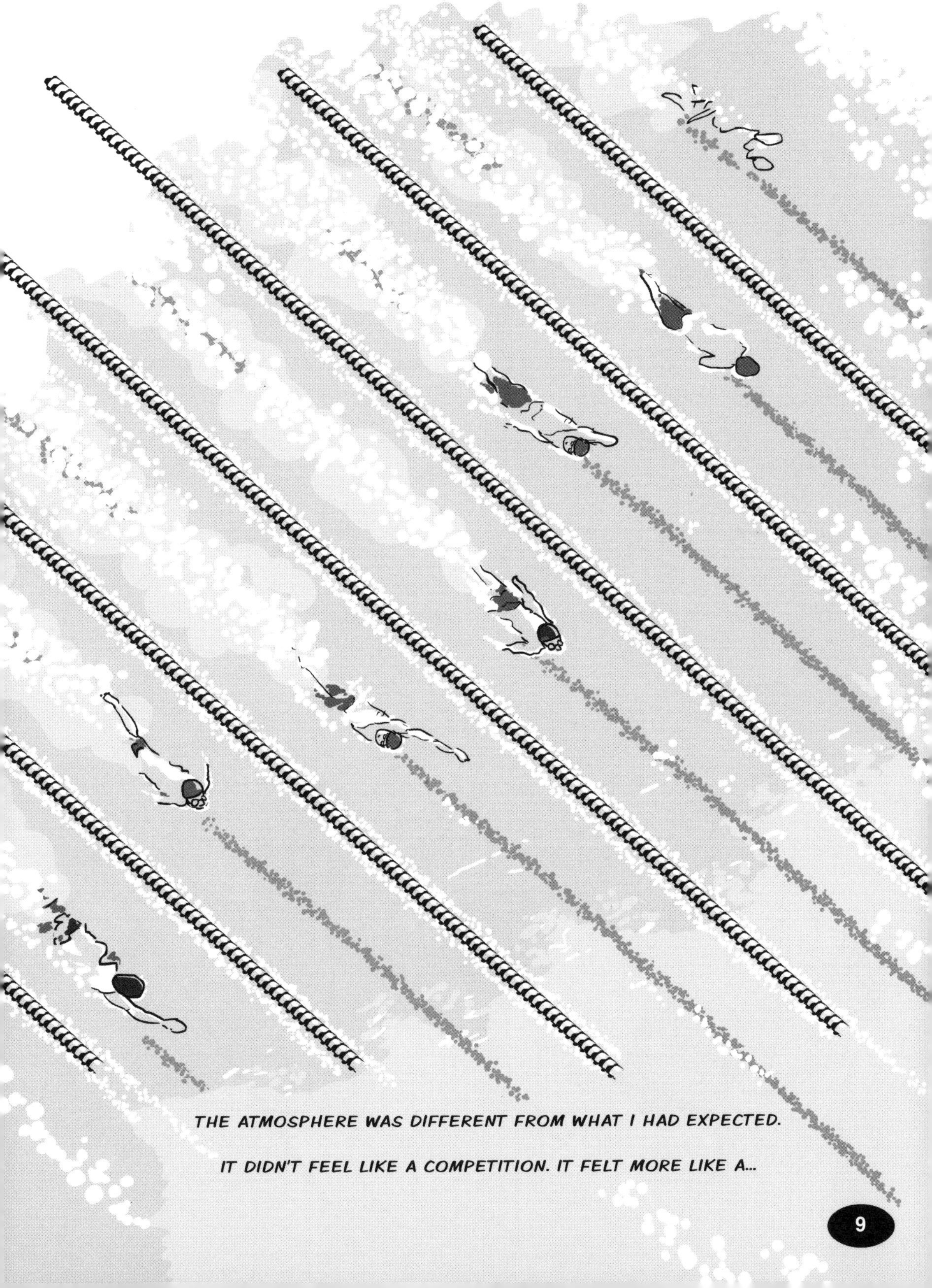

...CELEBRATION!
WE DIDN'T HAVE A BIG AUDIENCE IN THE STADIUM. AFTER ALL, THIS WAS NOT CRICKET! THIS WAS PARA-SWIMMING.
BUT THAT DIDN'T MEAN WE DIDN'T HAVE SUPPORT OR CHEERS...

...BECAUSE EVERY ATHLETE THERE CHEERED FOR EVERYONE ELSE.
I HAD NEVER EXPERIENCED ANYTHING LIKE IT BEFORE!
FOR THE FIRST TIME, I FELT I WAS NOT IN THE MINORITY.
LET'S GO!!!

100M BACKSTROKE
AND FREESTYLE
- THOSE WERE MY EVENTS.

I HAD QUALIFIED FOR THE FINAL ROUND WITH EASE, WHICH GAVE ME A LOT OF CONFIDENCE.

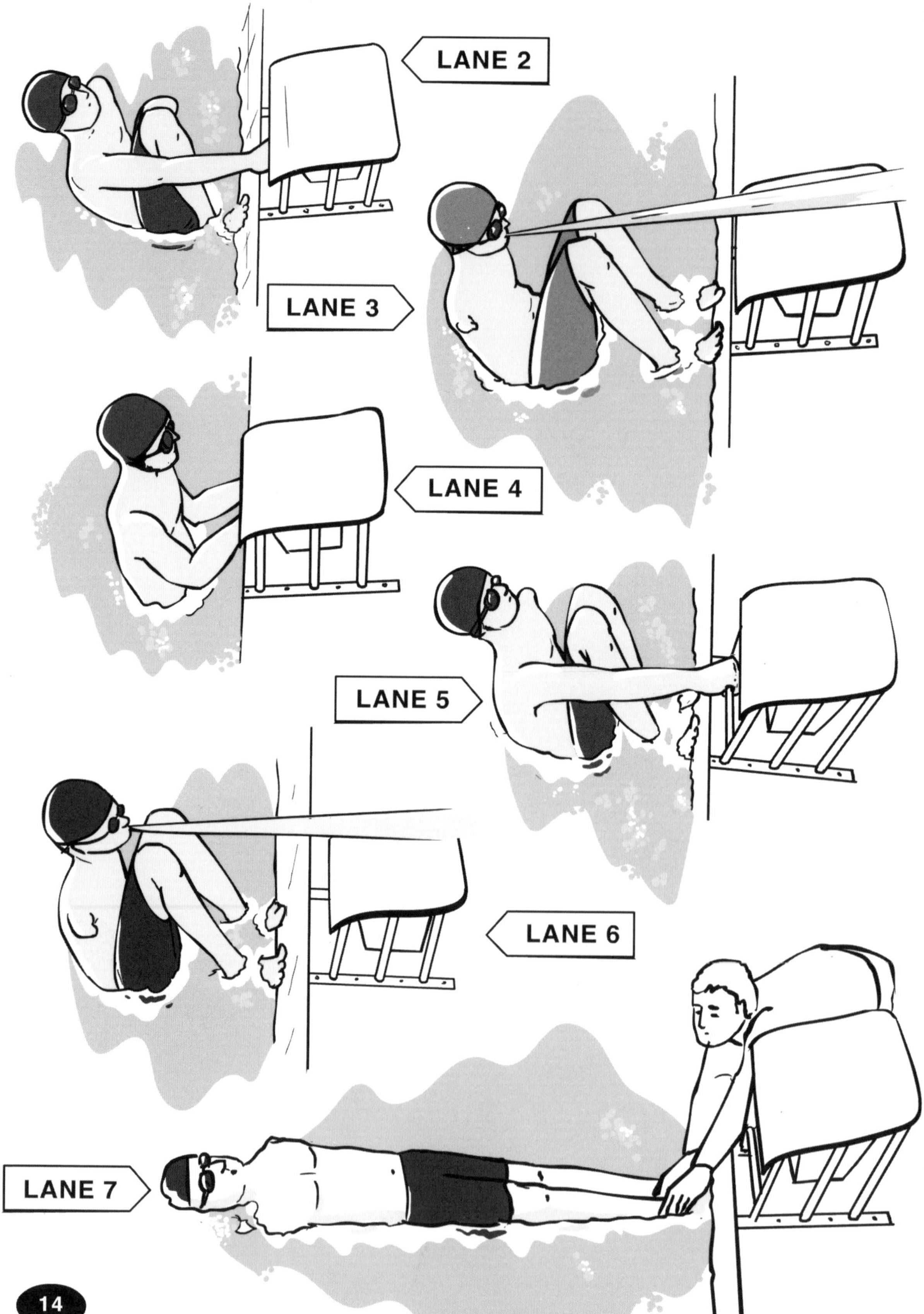
LANE 2
LANE 3
LANE 4
LANE 5
LANE 6
LANE 7

HOLD IT
TIGHT.
GOT IT?
MMM...

BANG
SPLASH

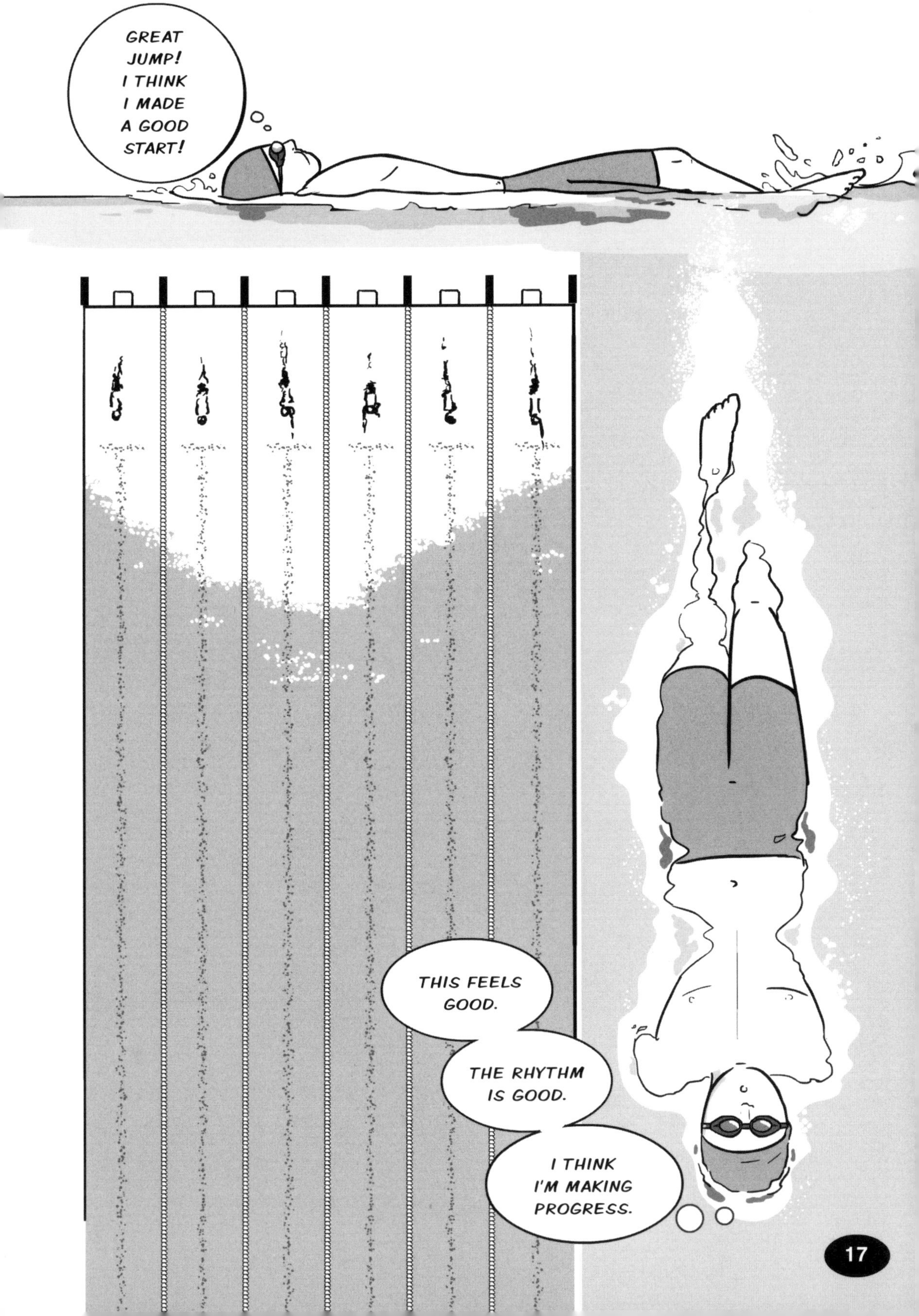
GREAT JUMP! I THINK I MADE A GOOD START!
THIS FEELS GOOD.
THE RHYTHM IS GOOD.
I THINK I'M MAKING PROGRESS.

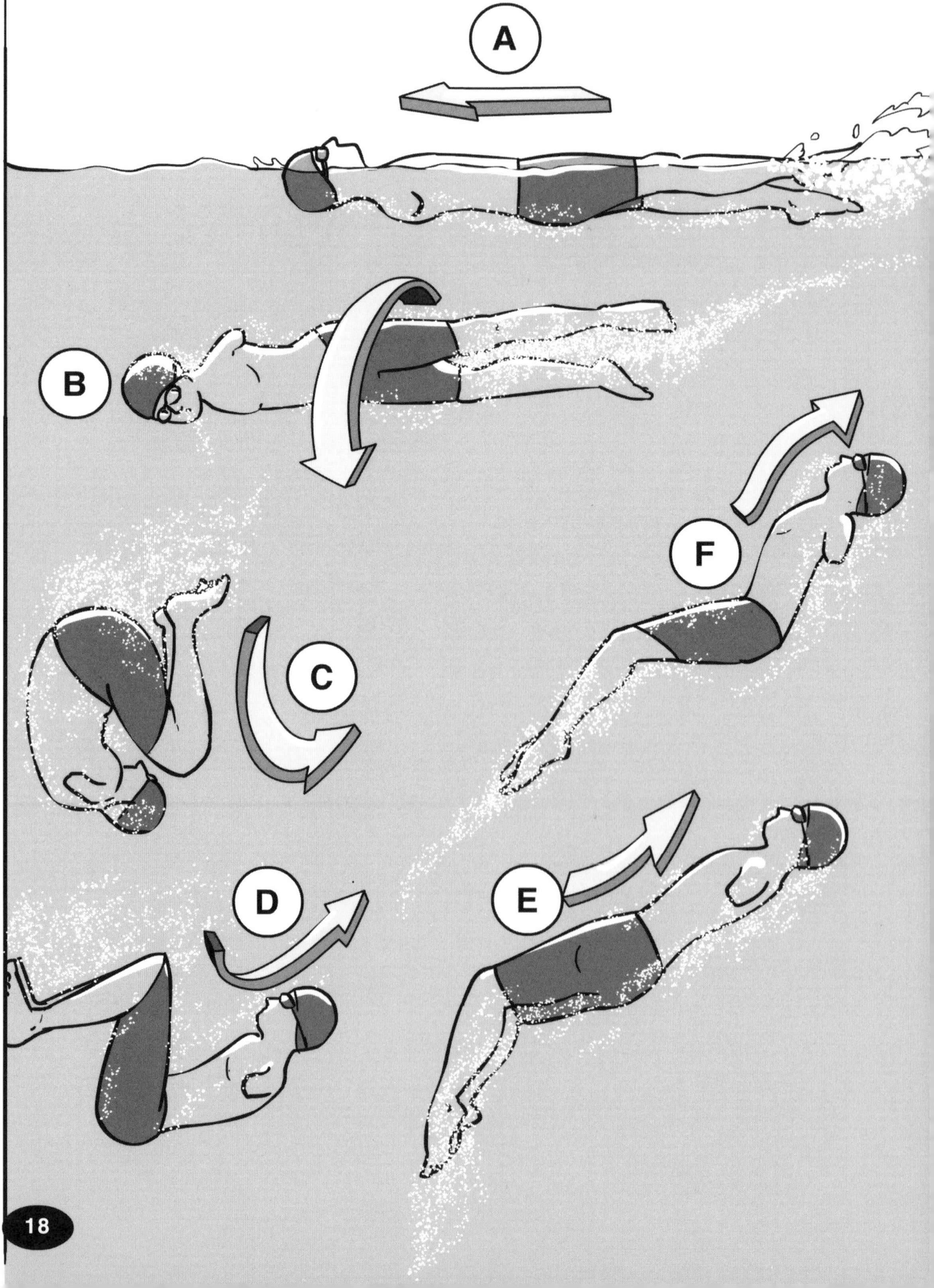
A
B
C
D
E
F

G
THAT TURN WAS GOOD, SMOOTH AND EFFICIENT.
MUST HAVE SHAVED OFF A FEW SECONDS...
BETTER THAN MY PRACTICE SESSIONS, SURELY.
I FELT CONFIDENT.
YES, THE WALL! JUST A FEW STROKES MORE!
MAYBE I'LL GET A MEDAL, ...GOLD,
OR AT LEAST SILVER...
FASTER...
...FASTER...
...FASTER!!
YESSSS!

BUT–
BRONZE
POSITION
4
VISHWAS
POSITION
I WAS PROBABLY A LITTLE TOO FOCUSED ON MYSELF.
I DIDN'T NOTICE MY COMPETITORS.

I WAS CRESTFALLEN.
GOOD!
PAT
COACH

GOOD?? COACH, I DIDN'T WIN. NOT EVEN A BRONZE!
THAT'S OK. YOU HAVE ONE MORE EVENT.
FREESTYLE FINAL
SILVER
BRONZE
POSITION
4 VISHWAS

TILL THAT POINT, I HAD BEEN SO ENGROSSED WITH MY PERFORMANCE THAT THE DESIRE TO WIN HAD SHUT MY EYES TO LEARNING.

I THEN BEGAN TO OBSERVE EVERY MOVE OF THESE SKILLED ATHLETES.
THEIR BIG LEAPS.
THEIR SMOOTH ENTRIES INTO THE WATER.
THEIR POWERFUL STROKES...
...AND THE EFFICIENT MOVEMENT OF THEIR BODIES.
WHAT BETTER OPPORTUNITY COULD I GET TO LEARN!
DID YOU KNOW YOUR TIMINGS IN BOTH THE EVENTS WERE BETTER THAN IN YOUR PRACTICE SESSIONS?
REALLY?
SWIMMING IS ONE OF THOSE SPORTS WHERE YOU COMPETE WITH YOURSELF, BEFORE COMPETING WITH OTHERS.
IF YOUR TIMING GETS BETTER EVERY DAY, YOU WILL BE ON THE PODIUM SOON.
WINNING IS IMPORTANT, YES. BUT IMPROVING IS EVEN MORE IMPORTANT.
COACH

SCOOBAROO
SCUBA DIVING
All Days 11 A.M. - 4 P.M.
GOA'S BEST SCUBA!
'IMPROVING IS EVEN MORE IMPORTANT.'
THAT'S SO COOL!
YES, LIKE I SAID, THAT EVENT WAS AN IMPORTANT EXPERIENCE FOR ME.
BY LOSING IN THE COMPETITION, I GAINED MORE KNOWLEDGE OF THE SPORT.
I WONDER IF I WOULD HAVE LEARNT ANYTHING AT ALL IF I HAD WON.
LOOKING AT ALL THE MEDALS, I'M SURE IT WAS ONLY A MATTER OF TIME BEFORE YOU STARTED WINNING.
MMM... YES, MAYBE.

DO YOU ALWAYS PARTICIPATE IN ALL THE STROKES?
NOT JUST PARTICIPATE, HE HAS WON MEDALS IN EVERY COMPETITION.
EXCEPT THE FIRST ONE. AND MANY ARE BRONZE AND SILVER, REMEMBER?
SO WHAT? THOSE ARE STILL MEDALS - A PODIUM FINISH!
AND YOUR THREE SILVERS IN BELGAUM WERE GOOD ENOUGH TO TAKE YOU TO CANADA!
IT WAS NOT THE SILVER THAT TOOK ME TO CANADA, IT WAS MY TIMING.
WELL, IT'S ALL THE SAME TO US!

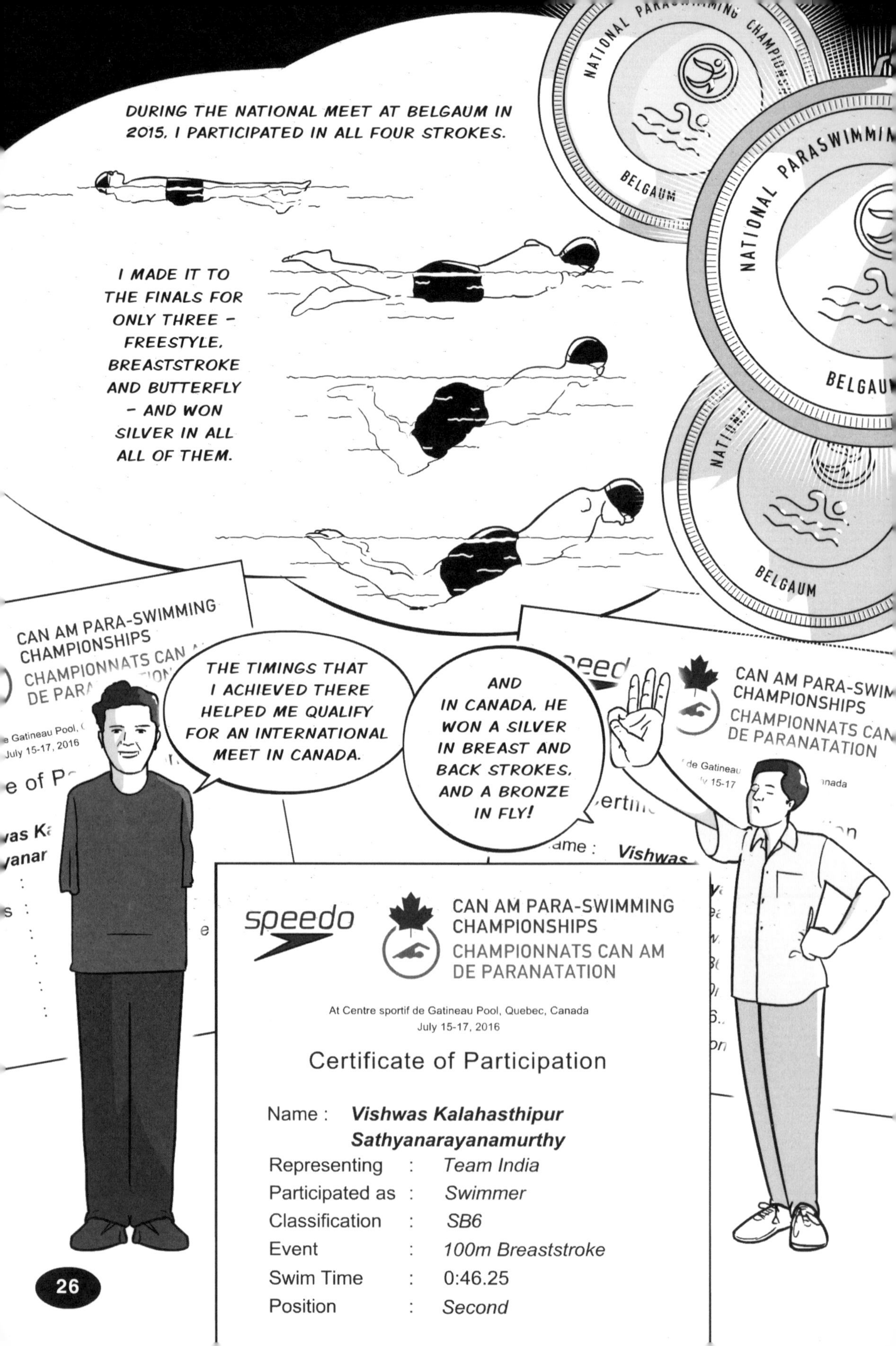

DURING THE NATIONAL MEET AT BELGAUM IN 2015, I PARTICIPATED IN ALL FOUR STROKES.
I MADE IT TO THE FINALS FOR ONLY THREE – FREESTYLE, BREASTSTROKE AND BUTTERFLY – AND WON SILVER IN ALL ALL OF THEM.
NATIONAL PARASWIMMING CHAMPIONSHIP
BELGAUM
THE TIMINGS THAT I ACHIEVED THERE HELPED ME QUALIFY FOR AN INTERNATIONAL MEET IN CANADA.
AND IN CANADA, HE WON A SILVER IN BREAST AND BACK STROKES, AND A BRONZE IN FLY!
speedo
CAN AM PARA-SWIMMING CHAMPIONSHIPS
CHAMPIONNATS CAN AM DE PARANATATION
At Centre sportif de Gatineau Pool, Quebec, Canada
July 15-17, 2016
Certificate of Participation
Name : Vishwas Kalahasthipur Sathyanarayanamurthy
Representing : Team India
Participated as : Swimmer
Classification : SB6
Event : 100m Breaststroke
Swim Time : 0:46.25
Position : Second

WHAT A THRILLING MOMENT THAT MUST HAVE BEEN!
YES, IT DEFINITELY WAS!
BUT, MORE IMPORTANTLY, IN THAT COMPETITION, I WAS GIVEN AN INTERNATIONAL CLASSIFICATION, S6.
WHAT'S THAT?
EVERY PARA-ATHLETE IS ASSIGNED A CATEGORY BASED ON THEIR PHYSICAL STRUCTURE AND THEIR DISADVANTAGES.
WITH ONLY TWO LIMBS, I WAS ASSIGNED TO S6.
I SEE. HOW IMPORTANT IS THAT?
OH, VERY!
WITH CATEGORIZATION, IT BECOMES A LEVEL PLAYING FIELD.
TILL THEN, I HAD HAD TO COMPETE AGAINST SWIMMERS OF ALL TYPES - SOME SIMILAR TO ME, SOME WHO HAD MORE ADVANTAGES, AND SOME WHO HAD LESS.
RIGHT, THAT IS IMPORTANT.

WELL? ARE YOU CONVINCED YET?
OI!
UFF, THIS GUY NEEDS TO STOP THIS.
I'M MORE THAN CONVINCED!
I APOLOGIZE FOR DOUBTING YOU. IN FACT, WE ARE VERY HAPPY AND PROUD TO HAVE YOU HERE.
THANK YOU VERY MUCH.
WE'LL DEFINITELY TAKE YOU FOR THE DIVE...
...AND, AS A TOKEN OF OUR APPRECIATION OF YOUR ACHIEVEMENTS, WE WOULD LIKE TO OFFER THIS DIVE FOR FREE.
OH, THAT'S VERY GENEROUS! THANKS A BUNCH!
...AND THANKS TO YOU GUYS FOR ALL THE MARKETING!

EXCITED?
YES!!
GOOD.
HOPE YOU ALL
REMEMBER
THE INSTRUCTIONS.

A FEW SECONDS AFTER DIVING INTO THE WATER, YOU'LL FEEL A BIT OF UNEASINESS DUE TO THE WATER PRESSURE.
SOME OF YOU MAY EXPERIENCE BLOCKED EARS AND PAIN.
IF THAT HAPPENS, HOLD YOUR NOSTRILS LIKE THIS AND BLOW HARD.
WE'LL BE USING A FEW HAND SIGNALS TO COMMUNICATE.
VISHWAS, NOD YES OR NO WHEN I SIGNAL SOMETHING. I'LL BE SWIMMING NEXT TO YOU. SO, IF YOU NEED ANY ASSISTANCE, LIKE RELIEVING A BLOCKED EAR, I'LL HELP YOU OUT.
OK, GOT IT.
ALL SET?
YES!
GREAT! LET'S GO!

2

I'M VISHWAS.
I'M A MARTIAL ARTIST.

THE REACTION TO THAT WOULD GENERALLY BE...

AND AGAIN, MY FRIENDS WOULD COME TO MY RESCUE.

WELL, IT'S ALL THANKS TO MY MASTERS.
FAST... QUICK! QUICK!! COME ON! HIGH KNEES! HIGHER! HIGHER!!
WHAT ON EARTH ARE YOU DOING THERE?
WHERE'S THE LEG? WHY IS IT STUCK THERE?
DON'T LOOK DOWN AT YOUR LEG!!

WHAT'S THAT STANCE?!
IS THAT WHAT I TAUGHT YOU?!
SEE, NO BALANCE.
THUD

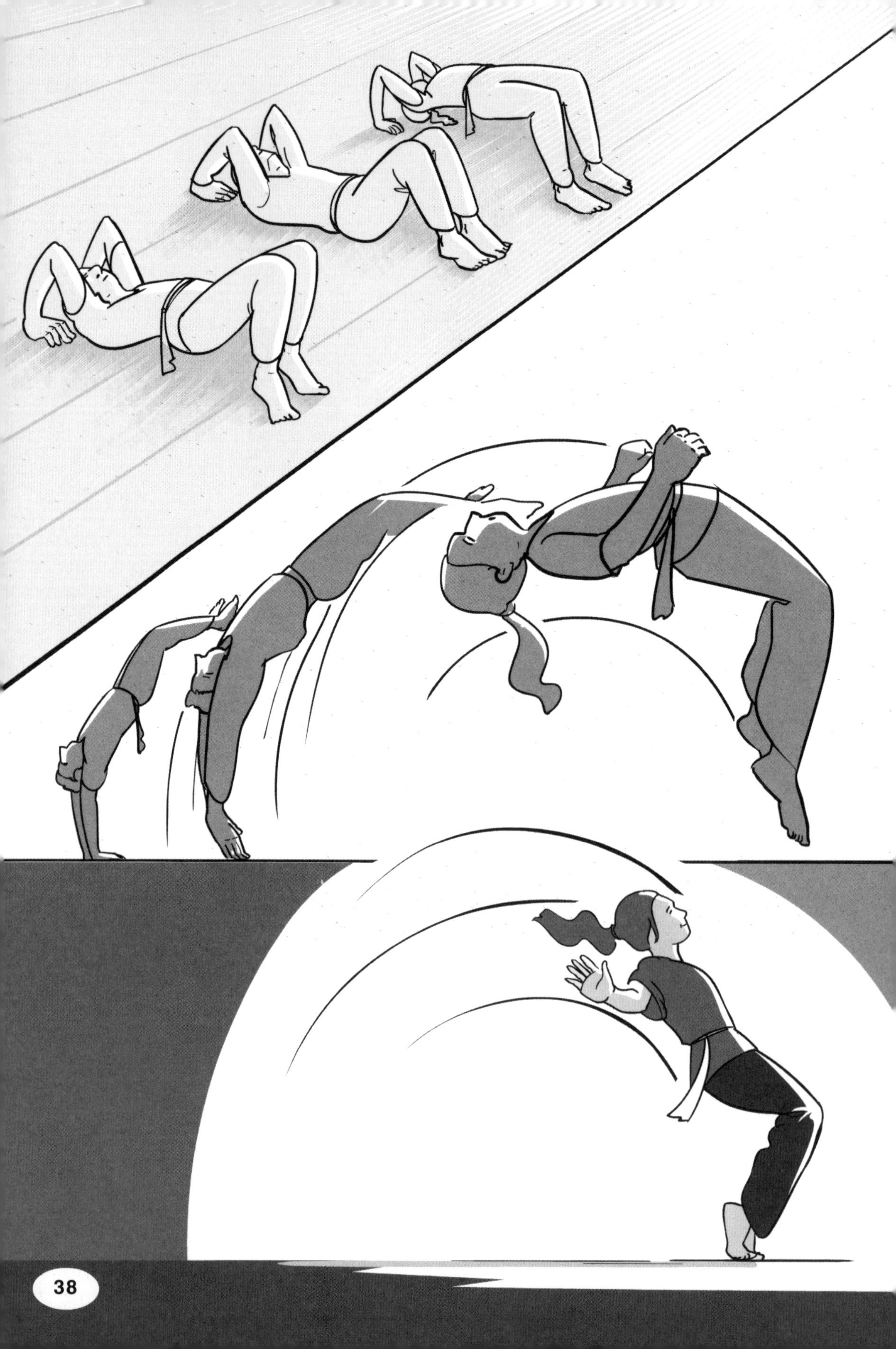

WOW!
YOU WANT TO DO THAT?
CAN I, RAMU SIR?
OF COURSE, YOU CAN!
REALLY? BUT HOW?!
HA! HERE, I'LL SHOW YOU.
THERE. THAT'S IT. SIMPLE.
THE KEY IS TO KEEP PRACTISING.
AND PRACTISE I DID.
ALRIGHT. LET'S BEGIN!

OWW!
OWW!
OWW!
OWW!

THAT ENCOURAGEMENT FROM MY SENIOR, RAMU SIR, GAVE ME THE CONFIDENCE THAT I COULD DO ANYTHING.

THE JOY ONE GETS FROM HAVING CONTROL OVER ONE'S BODY IS INDESCRIBABLE.

3

I'M VISHWAS.
I'M A DANCER.

THERE WERE THE USUAL REACTIONS.
?
!
DANCER? REALLY?!
TO WHICH I WOULD ALWAYS SAY -
DANCE IS NOT ABOUT MOVEMENT OR THE COSTUME. IT'S IN THE HEART.
I KNEW THAT LINE WOULD WORK! IT'S FROM A TELEGU MOVIE CALLED STYLE.
AND WE USED IT AS A THEME IN ONE OF MY PERFORMANCES.
WOW, THAT'S VERY PROFOUND.
SO WISE FOR YOUR AGE!

LET'S GO OVER THIS AGAIN, SHALL WE?
YES, MASTER!
THE CORE GROUP IS FIRST ON THE STAGE...
...AND AS THE MUSIC STARTS, WE BEGIN OUR PERFORMANCE.
AT THE FOURTH LINE OF THE SONG, I ENTER THE STAGE FROM THE LEFT.
I WATCH THEM UNTIL THE END OF THE FIRST DANCE.
THEN I ASK IF THEY CAN TEACH ME THE MOVES.

AT THIS POINT, I COME TO THE FRONT AND SAY -
'HOW CAN YOU DANCE?'
THEN I SHOW HIM MY MOVES AND ASK 'CAN YOU DO THIS?'
NEXT, I COME AND PERFORM MY STEP AND SAY 'HOW ABOUT THIS?'

I STEP IN AGAIN AND SAY 'YOU CAN'T DO ANY OF THIS. DON'T WASTE OUR TIME.'
AND I PUSH HIM DOWN.
I FALL DOWN AND START CRYING.

WE BOTH THEN ENTER THE STAGE AND HELP HIM GET UP.
ARGH!! SIDES! SIDES!! WHICH SIDE? ALWAYS MENTION THAT! HOW MANY TIMES HAVE I TOLD YOU ALL THIS?
SORRY, MASTER! I'LL BE ON HIS RIGHT.
AND I'LL BE ON HIS LEFT. THEN I SAY –
'DANCE IS NOT ABOUT MOVEMENT OR THE COSTUME. IT'S IN THE HEART.'
WHEN THE MUSIC STARTS AGAIN, WE TEACH HIM THE STEPS, FOUR COUNTS.
I FOLLOW THEM, TWICE. AFTER THAT, I DO MY SOLO TILL THE END.
THEN, WE ALL BOW, KNEEL AND APPLAUD!

GOOD. YOU HAVE ALL PRACTISED WELL! THERE'S NOTHING TO BE NERVOUS ABOUT.
NOW, HAVE FUN!
AND, OH, REMEMBER YOUR SPOTS!
OF COURSE, MASTER. DON'T WORRY!
GOOD EVENING EVERYBODY! WELCOME TO DANCE-DANCE. I'M YOUR HOST, AKUL BALAJI.
TODAY, WE HAVE A VERY SPECIAL PERFORMANCE BY A REMARKABLE PERSON.
WE'LL TALK ABOUT HIM AFTER THE ACT.
NOW, LET ME INVITE VISHWAS AND HIS TEAM ON STAGE!

WOOHOO! THAT WAS A WONDERFUL PERFORMANCE!
WELL DONE! REALLY BRILLIANT! I HAVE SEEN YOUR DANCE ON TV AND SOCIAL MEDIA. BUT THE FEELING, THE PLEASURE, THAT WE GET WATCHING YOU LIVE IS TOTALLY OUT OF THE WORLD!
I SECOND THAT! IT WAS JUST EXHILARATING! THE WHOLE CHOREOGRAPHY FITS THE THEME SO WELL! A HUGE ROUND OF APPLAUSE TO THE MASTER!
THANK YOU, SIR, MADAM.
THOSE ARE SOME WONDERFUL WORDS OF APPRECIATION FROM THE JUDGES.

VISHWAS, BRILLIANT! I'M A FAN FROM THIS MOMENT!
IT'S SUCH A JOY TO WATCH YOU PERFORM. HOW DO YOU FEEL?
THANK YOU, AKUL SIR. I FEEL VERY HAPPY.
TO GET AN OPPORTUNITY TO DANCE IS ALWAYS WONDERFUL.
BUT TO GET TO PERFORM FOR A PRESTIGIOUS TV CHANNEL LIKE THIS MAKES IT EVEN MORE SPECIAL.
I THANK SUVARNA CHANNEL FOR MAKING THIS HAPPEN FOR ME.
OF COURSE. SUVARNA CHANNEL IS DELIGHTED TO HAVE YOU HERE!
I ALSO WANT TO THANK MY MASTER AND THE GROUP. WITHOUT THEM, THE ESSENCE OF THIS THEME WOULDN'T HAVE COME OUT AT ALL.
YES, IT'S ALWAYS TEAMWORK, ISN'T IT? A BIG ROUND OF APPLAUSE TO THEM AS WELL!
SO, VISHWAS. TELL US A BIT ABOUT YOURSELF.

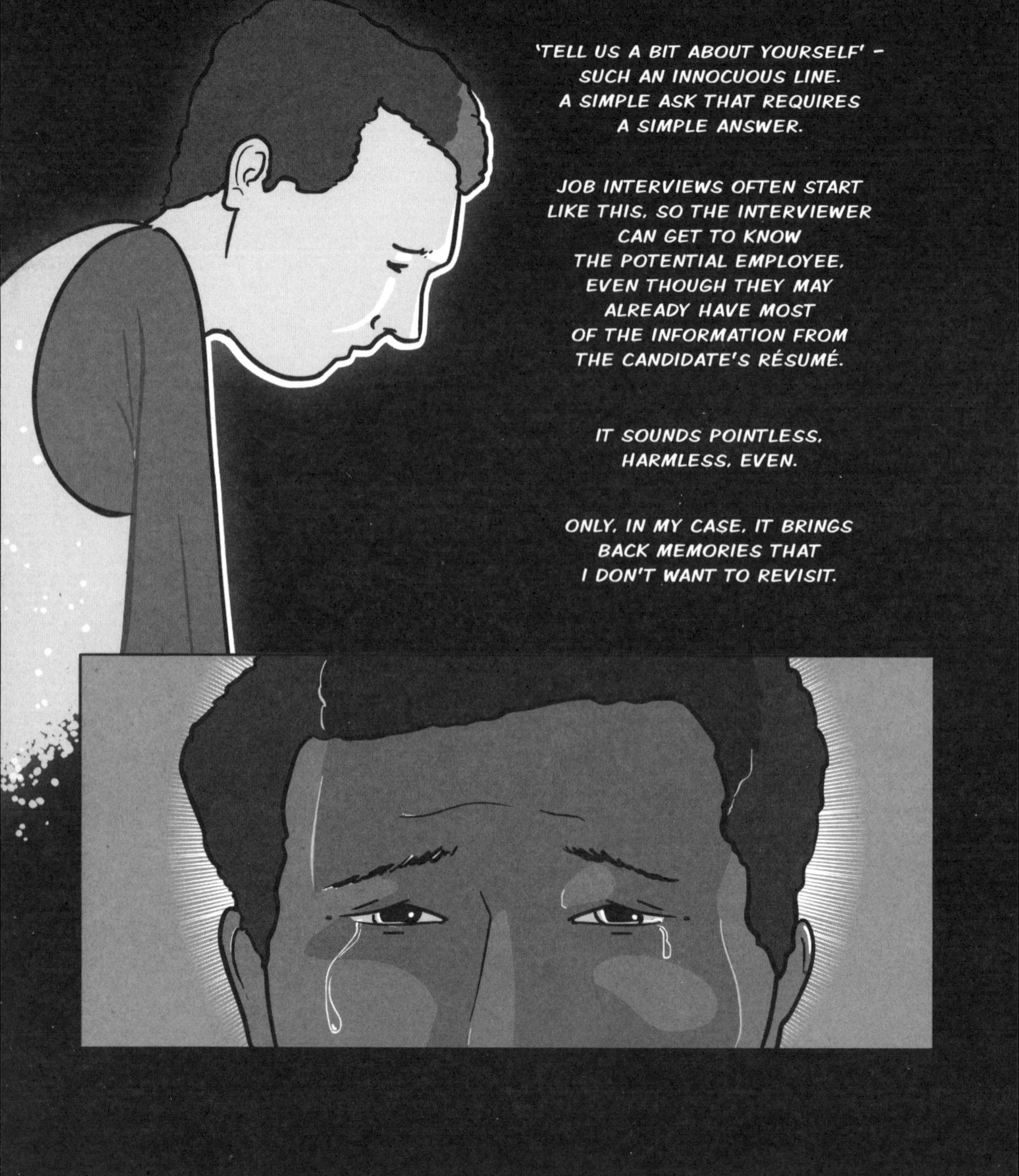
'TELL US A BIT ABOUT YOURSELF' – SUCH AN INNOCUOUS LINE. A SIMPLE ASK THAT REQUIRES A SIMPLE ANSWER.
JOB INTERVIEWS OFTEN START LIKE THIS, SO THE INTERVIEWER CAN GET TO KNOW THE POTENTIAL EMPLOYEE, EVEN THOUGH THEY MAY ALREADY HAVE MOST OF THE INFORMATION FROM THE CANDIDATE'S RÉSUMÉ.
IT SOUNDS POINTLESS, HARMLESS, EVEN.
ONLY, IN MY CASE, IT BRINGS BACK MEMORIES THAT I DON'T WANT TO REVISIT.

4

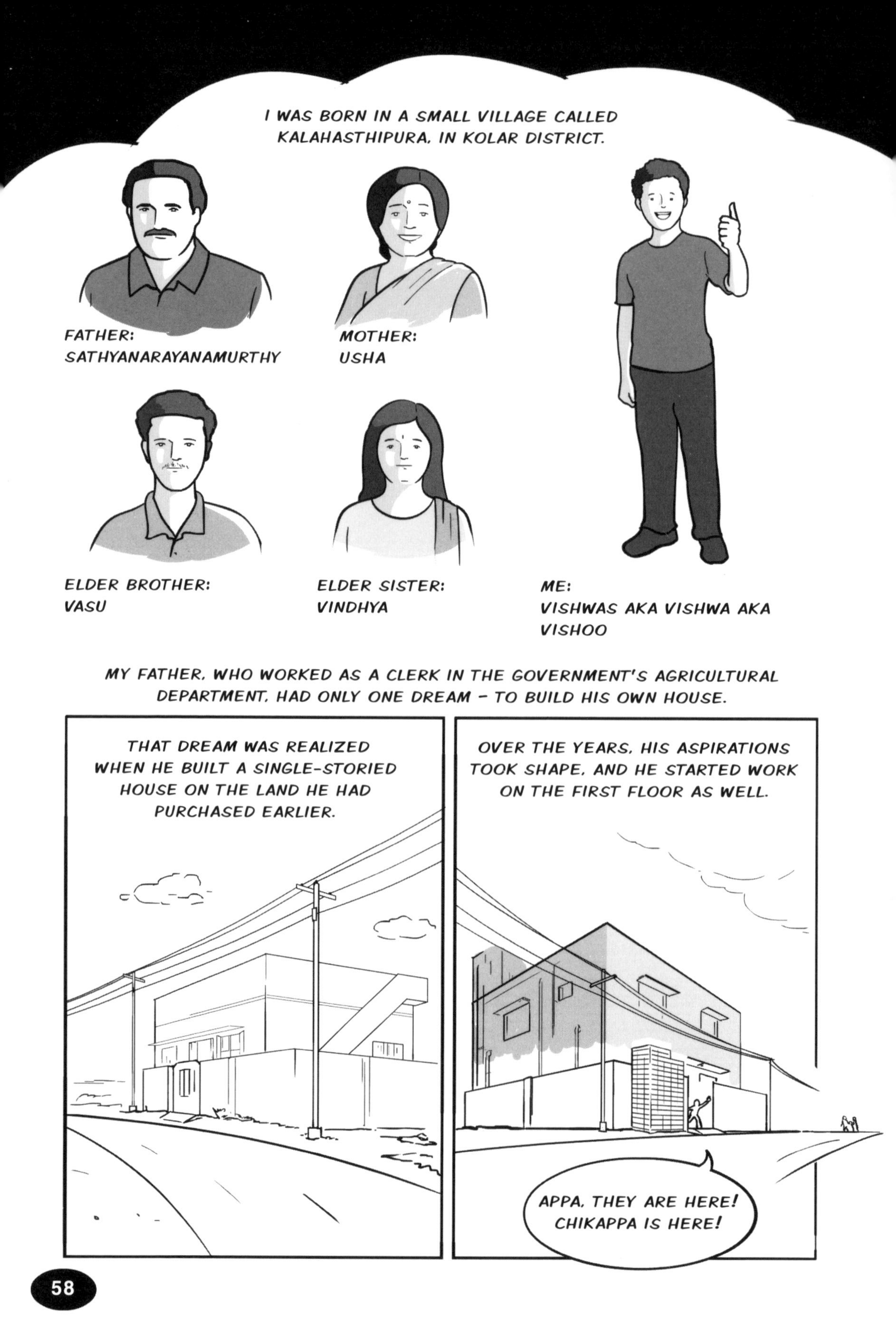
I WAS BORN IN A SMALL VILLAGE CALLED KALAHASTHIPURA, IN KOLAR DISTRICT.
FATHER: SATHYANARAYANAMURTHY
MOTHER: USHA
ELDER BROTHER: VASU
ELDER SISTER: VINDHYA
ME: VISHWAS AKA VISHWA AKA VISHOO
MY FATHER, WHO WORKED AS A CLERK IN THE GOVERNMENT'S AGRICULTURAL DEPARTMENT, HAD ONLY ONE DREAM - TO BUILD HIS OWN HOUSE.
THAT DREAM WAS REALIZED WHEN HE BUILT A SINGLE-STORIED HOUSE ON THE LAND HE HAD PURCHASED EARLIER.
OVER THE YEARS, HIS ASPIRATIONS TOOK SHAPE, AND HE STARTED WORK ON THE FIRST FLOOR AS WELL.
APPA, THEY ARE HERE! CHIKAPPA IS HERE!

WELCOME, WELCOME.
HELLO, ANNA.
HI VISHWA! HOW ARE YOU?

AREN'T THE WIRES TOO CLOSE, ANNA? IT DIDN'T MATTER EARLIER, WITH ONLY THE GROUND FLOOR. BUT NOW, IT'S VERY CLOSE TO THE FIRST FLOOR.
YES, I'VE RAISED A COMPLAINT WITH THE ELECTRICITY BOARD. I'VE BEEN FOLLOWING IT UP WITH THEM. THEY SAID THEY WOULD LOOK INTO IT.
HOPE THEY GET THIS DONE SOON.
YES, I HOPE SO.
HEY WAIT, I'LL CALL MY FRIENDS HERE.

THIS CONSTRUCTION WORK MUST BE CONSUMING ALL YOUR TIME.
YES. FORTUNATELY, THE ELDER ONE HELPS ME WITH SOME THINGS. SO, I'M ABLE TO MANAGE.
HA HA! YOU ALL ARE TOO SLOW FOR ME!

VISHWAS! STOP RUNNING AROUND INSIDE THE HOUSE LIKE THIS! GO ON, TAKE EVERYONE AND WATER THOSE NEWLY CEMENTED WALLS.

NORMALLY, MY FATHER WOULD'VE HAD TO ASK MORE THAN ONCE TO MAKE ME DO THE JOB. I WOULD OFTEN RUN AWAY TO PLAY WITH MY FRIENDS. BUT ON THAT DAY, I HAD COMPANY. AS MY COUSIN AND FRIENDS WERE WITH ME, I DECIDED TO FOLLOW MY FATHER'S ORDER PROMPTLY.

I TRIED TO REACH OUT AS MUCH AS POSSIBLE WITH AN AIM TO COVER EVERY PART OF THE WALL.
NOT A WISE MOVE FOR A FRISKY 10-YEAR-OLD.
OOPS!

NEXT THING I KNEW, I WAS NOT IN A FAMILIAR PLACE.

THE NURSE HAD TO SEDATE ME TO CALM ME DOWN. I FELL ASLEEP.

WHEN I WOKE UP AGAIN, I SAW MY MOTHER, BROTHER AND SISTER...
...AND, OF COURSE, THE DOCTOR.
I FELT AN INSTANT SENSE OF RELIEF LOOKING AT THEM. BUT THEIR FACES WERE TEAR-STAINED, AND THEY LOOKED DISTRESSED.
VISHWA!
AMMA, WHAT HAPPENED? WHY AM I NOT ABLE TO MOVE?
DO YOU KNOW WHERE YOU ARE NOW?
MMM, HOSPITAL?
YES, AT ST. JOHN'S HOSPITAL IN BANGALORE. DO YOU KNOW WHY YOU ARE HERE?
THE LAST MEMORY I HAD WAS OF PLAYING WITH MY COUSIN AND FRIENDS. I COULDN'T REMEMBER ANYTHING AFTER THAT.
MMM, NO.

YOU WERE ON THE TERRACE OF YOUR HOUSE AND MISSED YOUR FOOTING.
YOU FELL ON THE ELECTRIC WIRE, AND YOU WERE HANGING FROM THERE.
I REMEMBERED THE WIRES RUNNING NEXT TO MY HOUSE. BUT I STILL DIDN'T KNOW WHY I WAS IN THE HOSPITAL.
THE ELECTRIC CURRENT PASSED THROUGH YOU AND SEVERELY DAMAGED YOUR BODY...
...ESPECIALLY YOUR ARMS.
I COULDN'T GET MY HEAD AROUND WHAT THE DOCTOR WAS SAYING.
I LOOKED AT MY MOTHER, BROTHER AND SISTER. THEIR GRIEF-STRICKEN FACES HADN'T CHANGED.
I'M AWAKE NOW, ANYWAY. WHY ARE THEY STILL LOOKING GLOOMY?!

THE CURRENT ACTUALLY BURNT YOUR ARMS.
SO, WE HAD TO AMPUTATE ONE AND WILL PROBABLY HAVE TO AMPUTATE THE OTHER AS WELL.
AM... AMPU...?
AMPUTATION. THAT MEANS... ...ER... ...WE HAD TO CUT OFF YOUR RIGHT ARM.
WHA...?
HUH...?
HA HA HA HA HA HA
THAT REACTION IS A MYSTERY TO ME EVEN TODAY.
I'M SURE MY FAMILY THOUGHT THAT I MUST HAVE INJURED MY HEAD AS WELL.
THEN WITH ALL MY MIGHT, I TURNED TO LOOK AT MY RIGHT ARM...

...I COULDN'T FIND IT.
WHAT??!
NO! NO!! NO!!!
I WAILED. I CRIED. AND THEN REMEMBERED WHAT THE DOCTOR HAD SAID.
...WILL PROBABLY HAVE TO AMPUTATE THE OTHER AS WELL.
I FELT A SHUDDER PASS THROUGH ME. IT LEFT ME TREMBLING.
SCARED, I TURNED MY HEAD TO MY LEFT.

I SAW A CHARRED, BLACK ARM
RESTING ON THE BED.

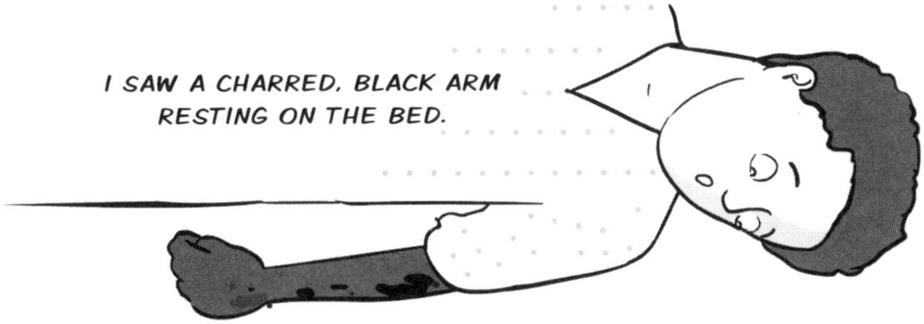

I JUST COULDN'T RECOGNIZE IT AS MY OWN.

FOR THAT MATTER, I COULDN'T EVEN RECOGNIZE MY BODY AS MY OWN. LIKE THE DOCTOR HAD SAID, THE ELECTRIC CURRENT HAD SEVERELY DAMAGED MY ENTIRE BODY.

NOT KNOWING WHAT WOULD HAPPEN NEXT MADE IT ALL THE MORE SCARY.

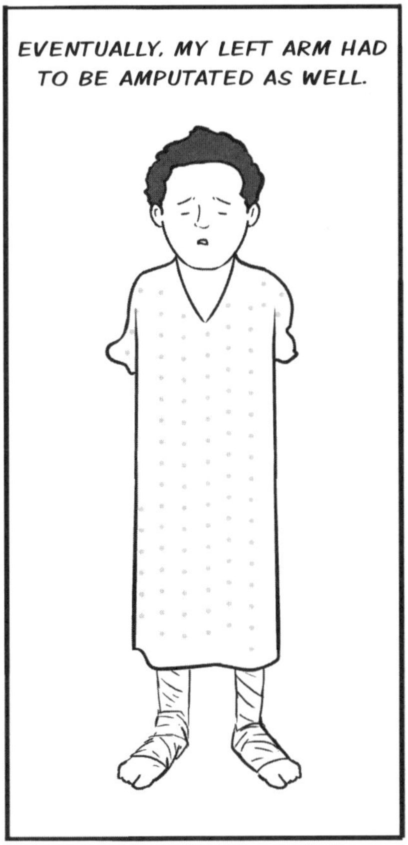

OVER THE NEXT FEW DAYS, I COULDN'T STOP CRYING – SOMETIMES THINKING ABOUT THE LOSS OF MY ARMS,

SOMETIMES BECAUSE OF THE PAIN ALL OVER MY BODY.
SOMETIMES BECAUSE I MISSED MY FATHER...

...AND SOMETIMES BECAUSE, WELL, I THINK IT JUST BECAME MY DEFAULT STATE.

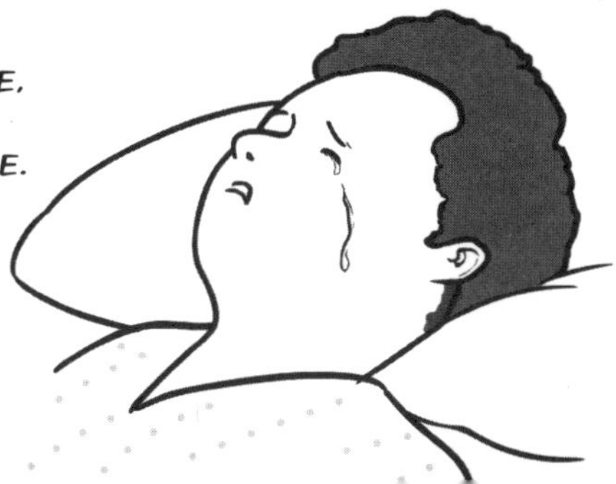

AFTER A FEW WEEKS, I WAS MOVED TO A HOSPITAL IN KOLAR TO CONTINUE THE TREATMENT.

SO DID MY SCHOOL TEACHERS.
I WAS RELIEVED THAT THEY DIDN'T ASK ME ABOUT
MY HOMEWORK OR TALK ABOUT MY ACADEMIC PERFORMANCE.

WE'RE REALLY SORRY FOR YOUR LOSS.
DON'T WORRY ABOUT VISHWAS. WE'LL TAKE GOOD CARE OF HIM IN SCHOOL.
THANK YOU, MA'AM.
I WAS THRILLED TO SEE SOME OF MY CLOSE FRIENDS.
HEY, VISHWA. HOW ARE YOU?
FOR THE FIRST TIME IN DAYS, I FELT HAPPY. BUT THAT LASTED ONLY A FEW MINUTES.
WHEN ARE YOU COMING BACK? WE ARE WAITING FOR YOU.
DOES IT HURT A LOT? CAN YOU MOVE? CAN YOU WALK?
IT WAS HORRIBLE TO WATCH. YOU WERE ON THE WIRE FOR 20 MINUTES! MUST HAVE HURT A LOT, NO?
MY FATHER SAYS YOU MUST BE IN A LOT OF PAIN. WE PRAY FOR YOU EVERY DAY. HE SAYS YOU ARE VERY FORTUNATE TO BE ALIVE. WHEN YOUR FATHER FELL DOWN AND DIED, WE THOUGHT...
HUH? WHAT?
YOUR FATHER, WHEN HE DIED, WE THOU...
WHO SAID MY FATHER IS DEAD??
MY FATHER HAS GONE TO KASHI TO PRAY FOR ME!

NO! YOUR FATHER DIED WHEN HE TRIED TO SAVE YOU.
NO! THAT'S NOT TRUE!
DIDN'T YOU KNOW? HE RAN UP TO THE TERRACE TO SAVE YOU, BUT HE FELL DOWN FROM THERE AND DIED.
NO!
NO!
NO!
WHAT ARE YOU TALKING ABOUT?!
AMMA!
AMMA!!
WHAT HAPPENED?!
VISHWA, WHAT HAPPENED? ARE YOU IN PAIN?
AMMA, THESE BOYS ARE SAYING APPA IS DEAD.
HE HAS GONE TO KASHI, RIGHT?
YOU BOYS GO NOW. YOUR TEACHERS ARE WAITING FOR YOU.
TELL ME, AMMA. WHERE IS HE?

IN ALL THOSE DAYS IN THE HOSPITAL, MY FAMILY NEVER SPOKE IN DETAIL ABOUT THE ACCIDENT.

BUT NOW, THEY HAD NO CHOICE BUT TO TELL ME EVERYTHING.

WE...
...WE WERE ALL INSIDE - YOUR FATHER, CHIKKAPPA, CHIKKAMMA AND ME.
WE COULD HEAR YOU ALL -
YOUR LAUGHTER, RUNNING AROUND AND PLAYING.
BUT SUDDENLY WE HEARD EVERYONE SCREAMING IN PANIC.
VISHWA! VISHWA!!

WE CAME RUNNING OUT.
WHAT HAPPENNED?
WHERE IS VISHWA?!
WH... WHAT?!
OH MY GOD!!!

YOU WERE DANGLING FROM THE WIRE.
VISHWA!
VISHWA!
CAN YOU HEAR US??
BUT YOU DIDN'T RESPOND.
WE THOUGHT YOU...
...YOU WERE...
YOU HAD LOST CONSCIOUSNESS.

NEIGHBOURS CAME RUNNING AFTER HEARING OUR SCREAMS.
OH NO! HOW DID THIS HAPPEN?
IS THAT SMOKE FROM HIS BODY?!
QUICK, SOMEBODY RUN TO THE EB OFFICE AND ALERT THEM! TELL THEM TO TURN THE POWER OFF!
VISHWA!!

AND YOUR FATHER, HE...
...HE RAN UP TO THE TERRACE.
AND WITH A WOODEN PLANK, HE TRIED TO KNOCK YOU OFF.
WHEN HE COULDN'T, HE STRETCHED TO REACH YOU.
BUT...

...HE LOST HIS BALANCE AND FELL TO THE GROUND.
YOU WERE STILL ON THE WIRE. WE DIDN'T KNOW WHAT TO DO.
EVENTUALLY, THE POWER WAS TURNED OFF, AND YOU FELL TO THE GROUND, RIGHT NEXT TO YOUR FATHER...
KRACK
THUD

...WHERE HE WAS LYING DEAD.

SHE WAS PROBABLY WAITING FOR THE 'RIGHT' MOMENT TO REVEAL THE TRUTH.
BUT WHAT WAS THE RIGHT MOMENT TO TELL
A 10-YEAR-OLD THAT HE HAD LOST HIS FATHER?
WHAT WAS THE RIGHT TIME TO TELL A YOUNG BOY
WHO HAD LOST HIS ARMS AND WAS IN UNBEARABLE PAIN?
HOW COULD ANYONE KNOW WHEN THAT RIGHT MOMENT WOULD BE?

IT'S UNIMAGINABLE, WHAT MY MOTHER WENT THROUGH –
TO WITNESS THE GRUESOME INCIDENT THAT TOOK AWAY HER HUSBAND
AND NEARLY KILLED HER YOUNGEST.

SHE HAD TO LIVE FOR TWO MONTHS WITH HER DOUBTS AND FEARS AND SOMEHOW
FIND IN HERSELF THE HOPE THAT I WOULD COME OUT OF THE COMA.

GUILT REPLACED MY PHYSICAL PAIN. I CRIED, INCONSOLABLY.

I SHOULDN'T HAVE GONE UP. WHY DID I DO THAT? IT'S ALL BECAUSE OF ME.
DON'T SAY THAT, VISHWA. DON'T THINK THAT WAY.
BECAUSE OF ME, IT'S ONLY BECAUSE OF ME. HE CAME TO SAVE ME. OTHERWISE WHY WOULD HE HAVE CLIMBED UP.
WHEN MY MOTHER COULDN'T FIND ANY MORE WAYS TO CONSOLE ME, SHE RESORTED TO THE AGE-OLD FALLBACK.
THERE'S NOBODY TO BLAME. YOU SHOULDN'T THINK THAT WAY.
WHO KNEW SUCH THINGS WOULD HAPPEN?
GOD ALWAYS HAS A PLAN.
IT'S ALL FATE.
THAT WAS NOT ENOUGH TO SOOTHE ME THOUGH.
APPA... APPA...
AND I'M CONVINCED THAT SHE DIDN'T BELIEVE ANY OF IT EITHER BACK THEN.

THROUGHOUT THE REST OF MY STAY IN THE HOSPITAL, I COULDN'T SHAKE OFF MY GUILT. I HAD FORGOTTEN HOW TO BE CHEERFUL. IF IT WERE NOT FOR MY MOTHER'S WILLPOWER AND FIGHTING SPIRIT, I WOULD PROBABLY HAVE ENDED UP WITH CLINICAL DEPRESSION.

I WAS YEARNING TO GO BACK HOME. I HAD BEEN AT THE HOSPITAL FOR NEARLY FOUR MONTHS. I STARTED THINKING ABOUT WHEN I COULD BE WITH MY FRIENDS AND SIBLINGS AGAIN, AND HOW SATISFYING THAT WOULD BE.

WHEN I GOT HOME, THE FIRST THING I NOTICED WAS THE ABSENCE OF THE WIRE.
HERE WE ARE!
AND THEN...
OI, OI, OI
WHY ARE YOU CRYING?
WE'RE BACK HOME NOW. OUR HOME.
YOU'LL FEEL BETTER SOON.
YOU CAN GO BACK TO SCHOOL AND SEE YOUR FRIENDS!
...MEMORIES OF MY FATHER CAME FLOODING IN ALL AT ONCE.
APPA...
OH VISHWA...
...YOU SHOULDN'T...

MY EXPERIENCE IN SCHOOL CHANGED AS WELL. LIKE:

- MY EXAMS WERE NOT WRITTEN ANYMORE, FOR OBVIOUS REASONS.

- I HAD TO RELY ON MY FRIENDS FOR EVERYTHING.

- AND MY TEACHERS WERE EXTRA CAUTIOUS WITH ME.
SIR, I WANT TO TAKE PART IN THE 100M RACE THIS YEAR TOO.
OH, ATHLETICS?
...MMM...
...THAT WOULD BE...
...ER...
WHY DON'T YOU PARTICIPATE IN A SINGING OR ACTING EVENT? OUR HOUSE DEFINITELY NEEDS MORE PARTICIPANTS THERE!
THEY DISCOURAGED ME FROM PLAYING DURING THE REGULAR PT CLASS, TOO.
INITIALLY, I WOULD JUST WATCH MY FRIENDS PLAY...
...BUT AFTER A WHILE, I PREFERRED SITTING INSIDE THE CLASSROOM.

I EVEN HAD TO STOP WHATEVER LITTLE I PLAYED WITH MY FRIENDS IN MY NEIGHBOURHOOD, BUT FOR A DIFFERENT REASON.

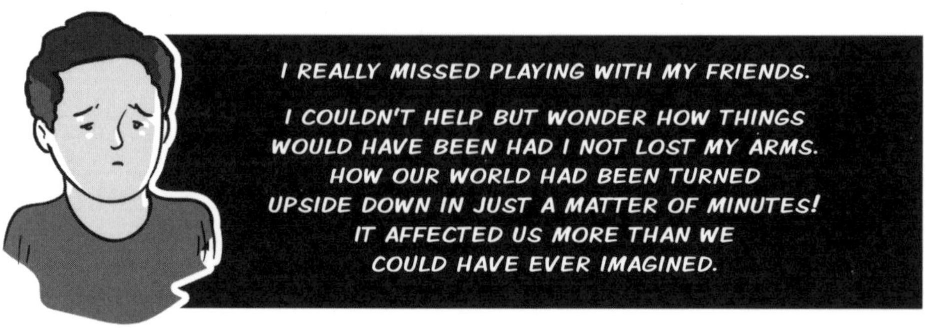

MY FATHER'S BROTHER HELPED US FULFIL MY FATHER'S DREAM OF BUILDING THE HOUSE. BUT WE WERE FAR FROM BEING IN A FRAME OF MIND WHERE WE COULD ENJOY IT.

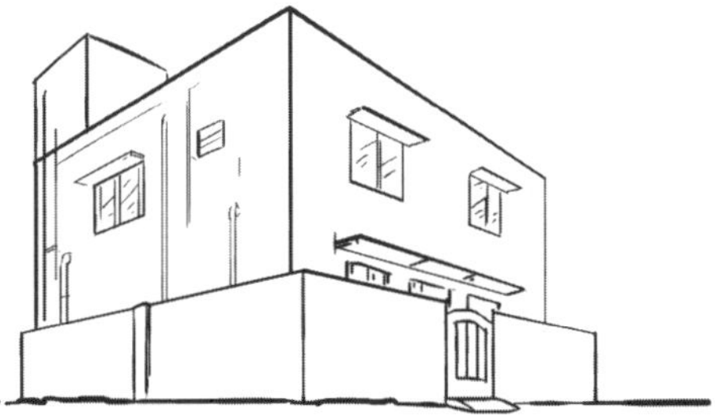

WE CONTINUED TO STAY ON THE GROUND FLOOR FOR THREE LONG YEARS. WHEN WE COULDN'T TAKE IT ANY LONGER, WE MOVED TO MY MATERNAL GRANDMOTHER SHAKUNTHALAMMA'S HOUSE IN BANGALORE.

FOR MY MOTHER, IT WAS A MUCH-NEEDED CHANGE.
WE WERE NOW PART OF A 12-MEMBER JOINT FAMILY.
SHE STOPPED FEELING LONELY.

I MADE FRIENDS. SOME VERY GOOD ONES, WHOM I CAN SAFELY CALL LIFELONG BUDDIES. BUT THAT WAS ONLY WHEN I WAS IN CLASS NINE. UNTIL THEN, IT WAS A NIGHTMARE.

OH, GOOD. YOU'RE BACK.
GO UP TO SEE GRANDMA. SHE WANTS TO GIVE YOU...
BATHROOM FIRST!
YOU DIDN'T GO TO THE BATHROOM IN THE SCHOOL? TODAY, TOO?
NO, I DIDN'T!
HOW LONG CAN YOU DO THIS? WHY DON'T YOU ASK YOUR FRIENDS FOR HELP?
I HAVE NO FRIENDS HERE! NOBODY WANTS TO BE MY FRIEND!
THAT'S NOT TRUE. THEY HELP YOU WITH TAKING NOTES?
YES.
THEN THEY ARE YOUR FRIENDS ALREADY. MAYBE NOT CLOSE FRIENDS YET.

I DREADED GOING TO SCHOOL. I WAS ASHAMED OF THE WAY I LOOKED. AN AVERAGE SCHOOL DAY ALWAYS STARTED WITH AN ARGUMENT BECAUSE OF THE NEW DRESS CODE I HAD ADOPTED SINCE MOVING TO BANGALORE.
IT'S OK, VISHWA. NOBODY IS GOING TO SAY ANYTHING.
NO, I WANT IT!
WON'T YOU FEEL HOT IN THE CLASSROOM?
DOESN'T MATTER. I'LL MANAGE.
YOU KNOW, SOMEDAY YOU'LL HAVE TO STOP WEARING THIS.
BUT I INTENDED TO WEAR IT FOREVER. NOTHING WOULD CONVINCE ME TO GET RID OF MY SHAWL, ESPECIALLY AFTER I REALIZED HOW INEFFECTIVE THE OTHER SOLUTIONS WERE.
AH, THIS IS GOOD. YES?
BUT WHAT CAN I DO WITH THIS?
!
FIFTEEN THOUSAND RUPEES DOWN THE DRAIN. JUST LIKE THAT. IT WAS HEAVY, UNCOMFORTABLE AND USELESS.
OH, EXCEPT WITH THE PROSTHETIC ARMS ON, I COULD FILL OUT THE SLEEVES OF A SHIRT.

THE SHAWL WAS MY PROTECTION. MY SHIELD. I FELT SAFE AND SECURE. WITH IT WRAPPED AROUND ME, I FELT I COULD HIDE MY 'SHORTCOMINGS' WHEN I STEPPED OUT OF THE HOUSE.
BUT IT WAS NOT ALWAYS ENOUGH. OFTEN, STRANGERS WOULD APPROACH ME AND SAY –
OOH, WHAT HAPPENED?
AWW... OH, YOU POOR THING.
THAT IS REALLY SAD!
YOU HAVE YOUR WHOLE LIFE AHEAD.
HOW ARE YOU GOING TO MANAGE?!
YOU POOR SOUL.
I JUST PRAY TO GOD THAT YOU...
SOMEHOW, AS A YOUNG BOY, SUCH REACTIONS DIDN'T BOTHER ME MUCH.

BUT I BEGAN TO FEEL TERRIBLE LISTENING TO THIS AS I GREW OLDER.
ESPECIALLY WHEN I SET OUT TO BECOME INDEPENDENT.

...FOLLOW ME EVERYWHERE.
GOOD EVENING, EVERYBODY! WELCOME TO DANCE-DANCE. I'M YOUR HOST, AKUL BALAJI.
SO, VISHWAS, TELL US A BIT ABOUT YOURSELF.
SUCH AN INNOCUOUS LINE. A SIMPLE ASK THAT REQUIRES A SIMPLE ANSWER. BUT FOR ME, IT BRINGS BACK MEMORIES THAT I DON'T REALLY WANT TO REVISIT.
I WAS BORN IN KOLAR. AT THE AGE OF 10, I LOST MY ARMS WHEN I FELL ON A HIGH-TENSION WIRE.
MY FATHER TRIED TO SAVE ME, BUT HE FELL AND LOST HIS LIFE.
MY FAMILY AND I MOVED TO BANGALORE. MY MOTHER HELPED ME BECOME INDEPENDENT.
TODAY, I'M A MARTIAL ARTIST WITH A RED BELT IN KUNG FU. I'M ALSO A TRAINED DANCER AND HAVE GIVEN MANY PERFORMANCES.
I'M A SWIMMER, TOO. I'VE COMPETED AT STATE AND NATIONAL LEVELS AND HAVE WON MANY MEDALS.
I'VE NOW QUALIFIED TO COMPETE AT AN INTERNATIONAL MEET IN CANADA IN THREE MONTHS.

BUT, IT WAS NOT EASY TO GET TO THIS LEVEL.
I HAVE FACED MANY REJECTIONS. EVERYWHERE I WENT, I WAS LOOKED AT WITH HORROR AND PITY.
ALL OF YOU APPLAUD AND ENCOURAGE ME NOW ONLY BECAUSE I'VE ACHIEVED ALL THIS.
IF YOU HADN'T KNOWN ABOUT MY ACHIEVEMENTS, YOU WOULDN'T HAVE SEEN ME BEYOND MY DISABILITY.
YOU PROBABLY WOULD'VE TREATED ME WITH PITY, TOO. AND THAT'S HOW EVERY PERSON WITH A DISABILITY IS TREATED.
IS IT WRONG FOR US TO EXPECT THAT YOU TREAT US THE SAME AS YOU TREAT OTHERS?
WHY IS THAT?
DO WE DESERVE ONLY PITY OR SYMPATHY?
DON'T WE DESERVE ANY RESPECT?
THAT CAME OUT OF NOWHERE. THE JUDGES WERE STUMPED. THE AUDIENCE WAS SHOCKED.
UNLIKE THE RECORDED AIRING OF THE SHOW WITH DRAMATIC MUSIC, THERE WAS PIN-DROP SILENCE IN THE STUDIO. TO THIS DAY, I DON'T KNOW WHAT PROMPTED ME TO SAY THOSE THINGS WITHOUT ANY PROVOCATION.

NO, VISHWAS. THAT'S NOT OUR INTENTION AT ALL.
WE COMPLETELY RESPECT YOU AND EVERYONE ELSE WITH DISABILITIES.
BUT THE WAY WE BEHAVE, PERHAPS, COMES ACROSS AS INSENSITIVE.
I DON'T THINK IT IS THE INTENTION OF ANYONE TO DISRESPECT YOU. I'M GLAD THAT YOU BROUGHT THIS UP.
WE CAN DEFINITELY UNDERSTAND YOUR POINT OF VIEW, AND I THINK IT'S TIME FOR EVERYONE TO ABSORB THIS AND CHANGE OUR ATTITUDE.
WE APOLOGIZE TO YOU FOR OUR INSENSITIVITY. WE DON'T WANT YOU, OUR STAR PERFORMER, OUR STAR GUEST, TO BE UNHAPPY.
WE HAVEN'T SEEN ANYONE WITH SUCH COURAGE AND GRIT ON OUR SHOW.
YOUR PARENTS WOULD HAVE BEEN PROUD OF YOU.
THEY COULDN'T HAVE CHOSEN A BETTER NAME FOR YOU.
VISHWAS, YOU ARE A WARRIOR!
I ONLY WISH MY MOTHER HAD BEEN ALIVE TO SEE WHAT I HAVE ACHIEVED.

5

I'M VISHWAS.
I'M A SURVIVOR.
I SURVIVED THE ACCIDENT.
I SURVIVED THE GUILT.
APPA!
I SURVIVED THE LONELINESS.
I SURVIVED, YES.
BUT THE EFFORT IT TOOK TO DO SO WAS NOT MINE ALONE.

ADVERSITY CAN TRANSFORM PEOPLE IN DIFFERENT WAYS.
IN THE CASE OF MY MOTHER, IT MADE HER STRONGER.
AS A SINGLE PARENT, SHE HAD NO CHOICE ANYWAY.
SINCE THE DAY OF THE ACCIDENT,
SHE DEDICATED ALL HER TIME AND ENERGY TO ME.
SOMETIMES, I WONDER IF MY SIBLINGS FELT IGNORED
OR IF SHE EVER FOUND THE TIME TO MOURN MY FATHER!

AS I GREW OLDER, SHE BEGAN TO HELP ME LESS.

NOT BECAUSE SHE COULDN'T OR DIDN'T WANT TO,
BUT BECAUSE SHE WANTED ME TO BE INDEPENDENT.

FOR SHE HAD THE SAME CONCERN ANY FAMILY MEMBER
OF A PERSON WITH DISABILITY WOULD HAVE -

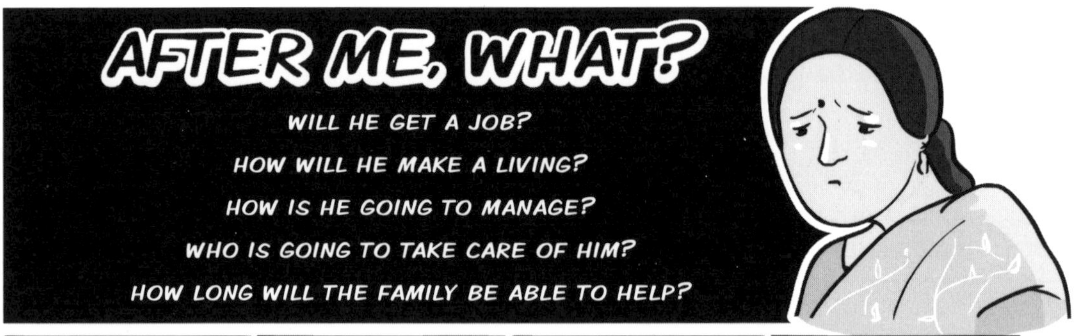

NO MATTER HOW MUCH REASSURANCE ONE GETS,
THESE ANXIETIES CAN CONSUME ONE'S PEACE.

WITH THE LACK OF A GOOD SUPPORT SYSTEM IN
THE COUNTRY, ONE CAN SAY THAT IT IS A CONCERN
WITH NO VISIBLE SOLUTION IN MOST CASES.

FOR MY MOTHER, THIS WORRY GREW IN MAGNITUDE
SOONER THAN SHE HAD EXPECTED.

DURING MY SECOND YEAR IN COLLEGE, MY MOTHER DEVELOPED A LUNG INFECTION.
HER CONDITION WAS SEVERE. IT WAS HARD TO WATCH HER SUFFER THROUGH IT.
BUT EVEN THEN, SHE HAD ONLY ONE THOUGHT.
HOW ARE YOUR PREPARATIONS FOR THE EXAMS?
GOING ON, MA.
DON'T LOSE FOCUS. YOU SHOULD THINK ABOUT WHAT YOU WANT TO DO AFTER GRADUATING.
HMM, YES. I STILL HAVE TIME FOR IT.
NO, NO. YOU SHOULD START LOOKING AT OPTIONS!
TALK TO PEOPLE AROUND. FIND OUT WHAT YOU CAN DO.
YOU NEED TO GET A GOOD JOB. NEED TO BE INDEPENDENT.
AND FOR THAT, YOU NEED A GOOD EDUCATION.
START YOUR PREPARATIONS RIGHT AWAY. YOU HAVE ONLY ONE YEAR LEFT!
ALAS, SHE HAD ONLY A FEW MONTHS LEFT.
DEATH CAME SOONER THAN WE HAD EXPECTED.

I WAS DEVASTATED.
I COULDN'T BELIEVE HOW RAPIDLY HER HEALTH DETERIORATED AND ABRUPTLY BROUGHT HER LIFE TO AN END.
I JUST COULDN'T COME TO TERMS WITH THE LOSS. SADNESS AND PAIN CONSUMED ME.
THERE WAS A VACUUM INSIDE ME. I HAD NO STRENGTH OR WILL TO DO ANYTHING.
I WAS NUMB AND DIDN'T WANT TO TALK TO ANYONE.
I REJECTED MY FRIENDS.
I REJECTED MY FAMILY.
I REJECTED MY LIFE.

SUCH WAS MY LACK OF INTEREST THAT ALL I WANTED TO DO WAS NOTHING.

I STOPPED GOING TO COLLEGE.

WITH MY SISTER MARRIED AND IN A DIFFERENT TOWN, AND MY BROTHER AWAY AT WORK EVERY DAY, I WOULD SPEND THE ENTIRE DAY ALONE.

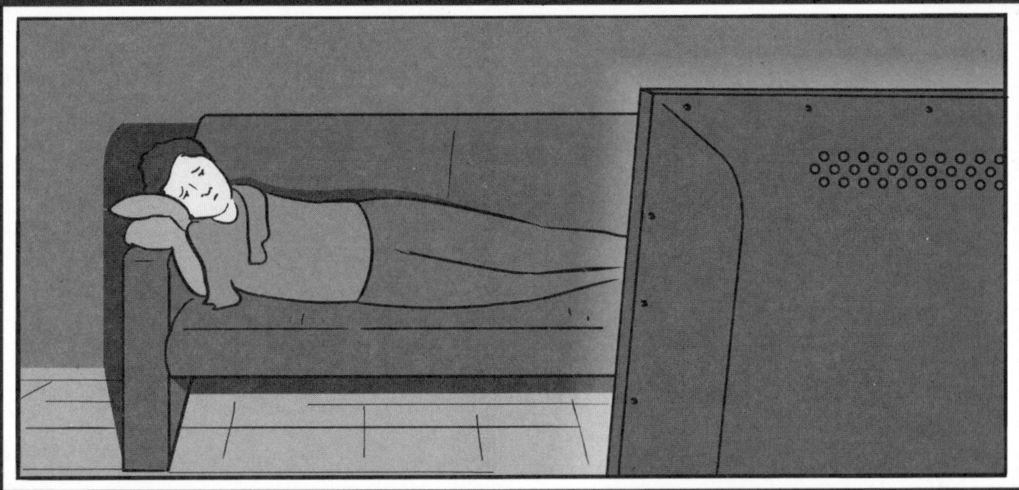

I WOULD WAKE UP AT 10.30 A.M., WATCH TV THROUGHOUT THE DAY WITHOUT REALLY KNOWING WHAT I WAS WATCHING, AND GO TO BED AT TWO OR THREE IN THE MORNING.

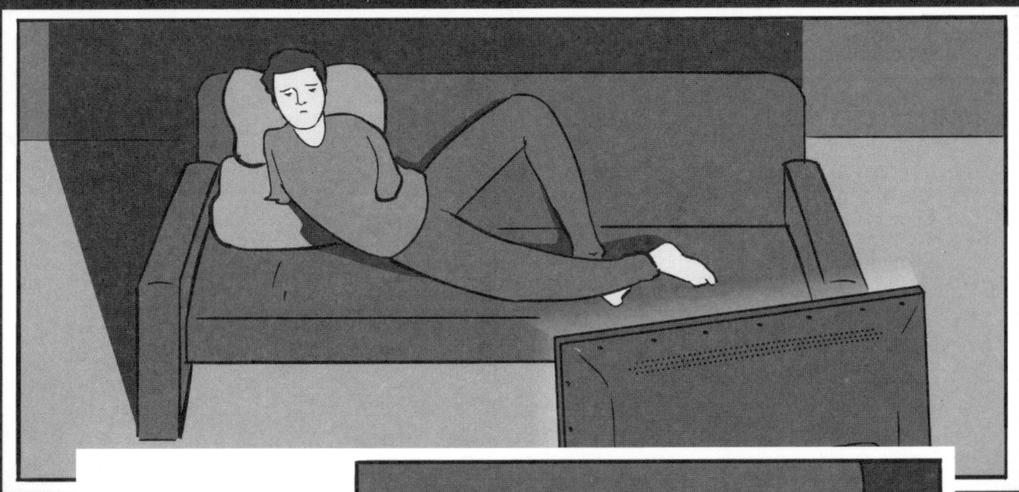

WHAT STARTED DUE TO DEPRESSION, JUST BECAME MY WAY OF LIFE.

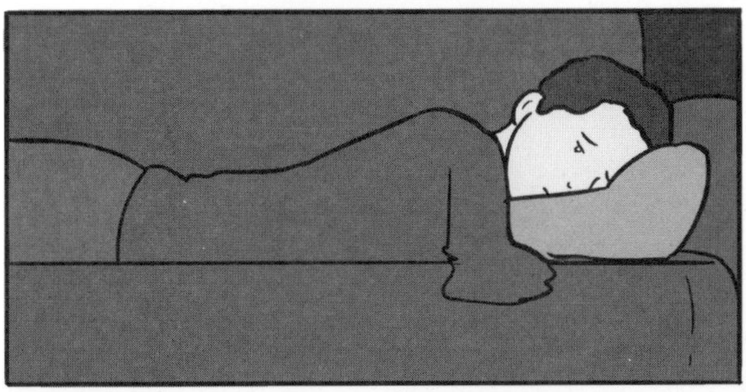

AN ENTIRE YEAR WENT BY LIKE THAT, UNTIL...

...I COULDN'T DO IT ANYMORE.

THAT PUSH BROUGHT ME OUT OF LETHARGY.

THAT PUSH BROUGHT ME BACK TO LIFE.

WITH A GREAT DEAL OF SUPPORT FROM MY FRIENDS AND PROFESSORS, I GRADUATED THAT YEAR, CLEARING ALL MY ARREARS.

ARMED WITH A B.COM CERTIFICATE,
I WAS NOW PLANNING FOR THE NEXT PHASE OF MY LIFE.
VISHWA! HERE, CALL THIS PERSON. I'VE SPOKEN TO HIM ABOUT YOU.
FIX AN INTERVIEW.
OH, THANK YOU, MAMA! I'LL DO THAT.
THIS IS GREAT! I CAN START EARNING NOW!
BUT-
OH! I DIDN'T KNOW ABOUT THIS... ...ER... ...YOUR CONDITION.
MANAGER
OK, TELL ME ABOUT YOURSELF.
WHAT HAPPENED TO YOU?
WERE YOU BORN THIS WAY?
HOW DO YOU MANAGE?
I FACED DIFFICULTIES AS A STUDENT BECAUSE OF MY DISABILITY.
BUT AT LEAST I DIDN'T HAVE TO REPEAT MY STORY EVERY DAY AND RELIVE THE PAST.
YOUR FATHER DIED TRYING TO SAVE YOU?!
AND NOW YOUR MOTHER! OH MY GOD.
OH MY GOD! THAT'S TERRIBLE.
I JUST FEEL FOR YOU!

BUT IT WAS THE SAME THERE, TOO.

I ATTENDED INTERVIEWS, EVEN THOUGH I EXPECTED TO BE REJECTED. ONLY HOPE KEPT ME GOING - THE HOPE THAT SOMEONE WOULD SEE PAST MY DISABILITY AND EMPLOY ME.

MEANWHILE, MY FRIENDS WERE FINDING JOBS.

AS THEY GOT BUSIER WITH THEIR CAREER, WE MET LESS AND LESS - FROM ONCE A WEEK, IT CHANGED TO ONCE A MONTH.

GRADUALLY THAT STOPPED AS WELL, AND WE ONLY CONNECTED OVER THE PHONE ONCE IN A WHILE.

I DID OPEN A MOBILE SHOP, BUT HAD TO CLOSE IT BECAUSE OF POOR SALES. PERHAPS I LACKED BUSINESS ACUMEN. I WAS BEGINNING TO FEEL LIKE A FAILURE.

IT FELT AS THOUGH THE WORLD WAS MOVING AHEAD WHILE I WAS STUCK IN THE SAME PLACE.

I WAS GETTING FRUSTRATED.
FRUSTRATION LED TO DEPRESSION, AND DEPRESSION LED TO LAZINESS.
BEFORE I REALIZED IT, I WAS SUCKED INTO THE SAME CYCLE AGAIN.
ANY INTERVIEW CALLS, VISHWA?
NO, ANNA.
DID YOU APPLY TO THAT NEW COMPANY I TOLD YOU ABOUT?
VISHWA!
VISHWA!
VISHWA!!
UH, SORRY, ANNA!
LOOK, HOW LONG CAN YOU BE LIKE THIS? YOU NEED TO DO SOMETHING ABOUT IT.
IT'S NOT THAT I WANTED TO LANGUISH LIKE THIS.
I JUST DIDN'T FEEL MOTIVATED ENOUGH TO DO ANYTHING.
FOR DAYS, I WAITED FOR A SPARK, A MOMENT OF INSPIRATION, TO GET ME OUT OF THIS.
LIKE IN THE MOVIES, WHERE A PROTAGONIST'S LIFE IMPROVES DRASTICALLY IN ONE SONG!
IF ONLY I HAD A JOB.
IF ONLY I HAD MY ARMS.
IF ONLY THE ACCIDENT HAD NOT HAPPENED.

I HAD ALWAYS BEEN ASHAMED OF THE WAY I LOOKED.
BUT NOW, I WAS ASHAMED OF MYSELF FOR THROWING AWAY MY MOTHER'S EFFORTS.

THAT WAS MY MOMENT OF INSPIRATION.

I HAD SUNK SO LOW THAT THE ONLY WAY OUT WAS UP.

AND I DID.

I CAME UP WITH A PLAN, A BIG PLAN THAT WOULD CHANGE MY LIFE FOREVER.

EVENTUALLY, I FOUND SOMETHING TO DO.

IT DIDN'T MATTER WHAT THE ACTIVITY WAS, AS LONG AS IT KEPT ME OCCUPIED.
I DIDN'T WANT TO BE IDLE ANYMORE.

WITH THAT BEING MY GOAL, I GRADUALLY TRIED VARIOUS OTHER THINGS.

ONE COULD SAY I BECAME MORE ADVENTUROUS.
SNIP
EVERY STEP REQUIRED A GREAT LEVEL OF DEXTERITY. BUT, NONE MORE THAN THE NEXT ONE.
HIGH
LOW
WOOOOSH
CLICK
I MUST ADMIT, IT WAS A BIT SCARY. BUT THE RESULT DEFINITELY WAS WORTH IT.
NOT THAT I COOKED ELABORATE MEALS, BUT THAT WAS NOT MY GOAL ANYWAY.
GULP
GULP
GULP
ALL THIS WAS NOT EASY.
IT TOOK TIME. BUT THAT WAS NOT A RESOURCE I WAS RUNNING SHORT OF.
OH, NO TOMATOES. I'LL GO UP AND GET SOME FROM PATTI.
OR...

HALF A KILO OF TOMATOES, PLEASE. MONEY IS IN THE BAG.
IT'S AMAZING WHAT THESE SMALL VICTORIES CAN DO FOR ONE'S CONFIDENCE.
I SHOULD STEP OUT MORE OFTEN. GET SOME FRESH AIR, INSTEAD OF SITTING INDOORS ALL THE TIME.
THE VERY NEXT MORNING, I HAD A NEW ACTIVITY TO START THE DAY.
WHILE THESE CHORES WOULD TAKE CARE OF MY MORNING HOURS, I STILL HAD THE REST OF THE DAY.
MMM...WHAT ELSE CAN I DO?

SRGM SRGM
POOR GUY.
WONDER HOW HE MANAGES.
VERY GOOD, VISHWAS. ONE MORE TIME.
THIS MUSIC CLASS, IT'S NOT WORKING FOR ME. I FIND IT VERY BORING.
MAYBE THIS PLACE IS NOT GOOD? TRY SOME OTHER PLACE THEN.
NO, NO. I'M UNABLE TO SIT STILL IN ONE PLACE AND DO IT.
OH, OK.
HEY! I'LL COME WITH YOU TOMORROW WHEN YOU GO FOR YOUR KUNG FU CLASS. I WANT TO EXPLORE THAT!
THAT'S NOT A BAD IDEA!
ACTUALLY, IT'S BRILLIANT. SHIFU WILL BE THRILLED!
I'LL TALK TO HIM ABOUT IT.

SO, YOUR FRIEND TELLS ME YOU WANT TO LEARN KUNG FU.
YES, SIR. I DON'T KNOW IF IT'S POSSIBLE. BUT I WANT TO TRY.
NOTHING'S IMPOSSIBLE. IN MARTIAL ARTS, THE ONLY OBSTACLE IS YOURSELF.
BUT, I WANT TO KNOW THIS - WHY DO YOU WANT TO LEARN?
MMM...I DON'T KNOW, SIR. I FEEL I NEED TO CHALLENGE MYSELF.
I FEEL I CAN DO A LOT IN SPITE OF MY DISABILITY.
I HAVE A LOT OF FRUSTRATION, SIR. AND I FEEL THIS WILL HELP ME VENT IT OUT.
ALRIGHT, YOU CAN START RIGHT AWAY.
BUT DON'T EXPECT ANY SPECIAL TREATMENT. EVERYONE'S EQUAL IN THIS CLASS.
YES, SHIFU!
FOR THE FIRST TIME, I FELT INCLUDED.

I WAS NOT GIVEN SPECIAL TREATMENT, BUT I WAS GIVEN SPECIAL ATTENTION - SINCE THEY COULD NOT TRAIN ME WITH THE USUAL METHODS.

THIS SPARRING SESSION WILL BE VERY DIFFERENT FOR YOU.
YOU CAN USE YOUR HANDS TO BLOCK HIS KICKS, BUT YOU'RE NOT ALLOWED TO PUNCH HIM.
YOU CAN ONLY USE KICKS TO MAKE THE ATTACK.
OK, SHIFU.
AND, VISHWAS, USE SWEEPS AND KICKS TO ATTACK AND DEFEND.
READY?
FIGHT!

SMACK
POW
COME ON, MOVE FASTER, FASTER!
DON'T JUST STAY IN ONE PLACE! MOVE AROUND!
IF YOU CAN'T BLOCK, AVOID IT! MOVE AWAY TO THE SIDE AND DODGE.
TAK
KRACK
AND USE A SPINNING BACK KICK! YOU WERE TAUGHT THAT, RIGHT?
THWACK
YES, SHIFU!
THEN USE IT!

MOMENTUM IS AN AMAZING THING.

ONCE YOU HAVE IT, IT GIVES YOU A FEELING OF POWER, WHICH IN TURN GIVES YOU CONFIDENCE.

AND THAT CONFIDENCE SPILLS OVER INTO EVERY PART OF YOUR LIFE.

I WANTED TO USE THE MOMENTUM I HAD TO MY ADVANTAGE.

I WANTED TO BE MORE ADVENTUROUS AND TRY NEW EXPERIENCES.

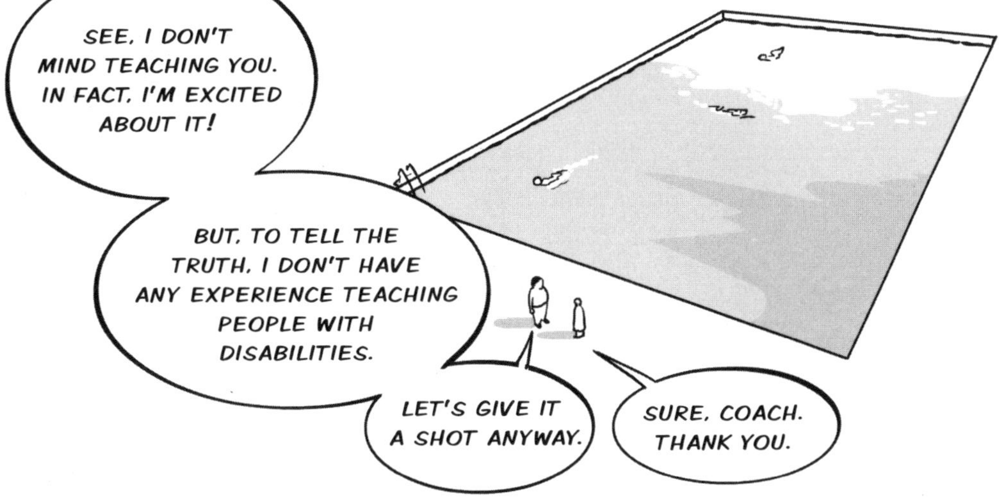

AND THIS IS HOW MY TRAINING STARTED IN SWIMMING.

I ENJOYED THE TRAINING THOROUGHLY AND DIDN'T MIND WAKING UP EARLY.
BUT, MY BROTHER, AND ON SOME DAYS, MY FRIENDS, HAD TO SACRIFICE THEIR SLEEP BECAUSE OF ME.
SORRY, ANNA, I KNOW IT'S TOO EARLY FOR YOU.
NO, THAT'S OK, VISHWA.
I DON'T MIND AT ALL.
AH, AGAIN, YOU ARE HERE EARLIER THAN ME!
GOOD MORNING, COACH!
VISHWAS, I'M ONLY NOW GETTING THE HANG OF IT AFTER TRAINING YOU FOR A WEEK.
YOU'LL NEED A LOT MORE TRAINING.
IN ADDITION TO YOUR ONE-HOUR CLASS, CAN YOU TRAIN WITH THE 6.30 A.M. BATCH TOO?
SURE, COACH. I CAN DO THAT.

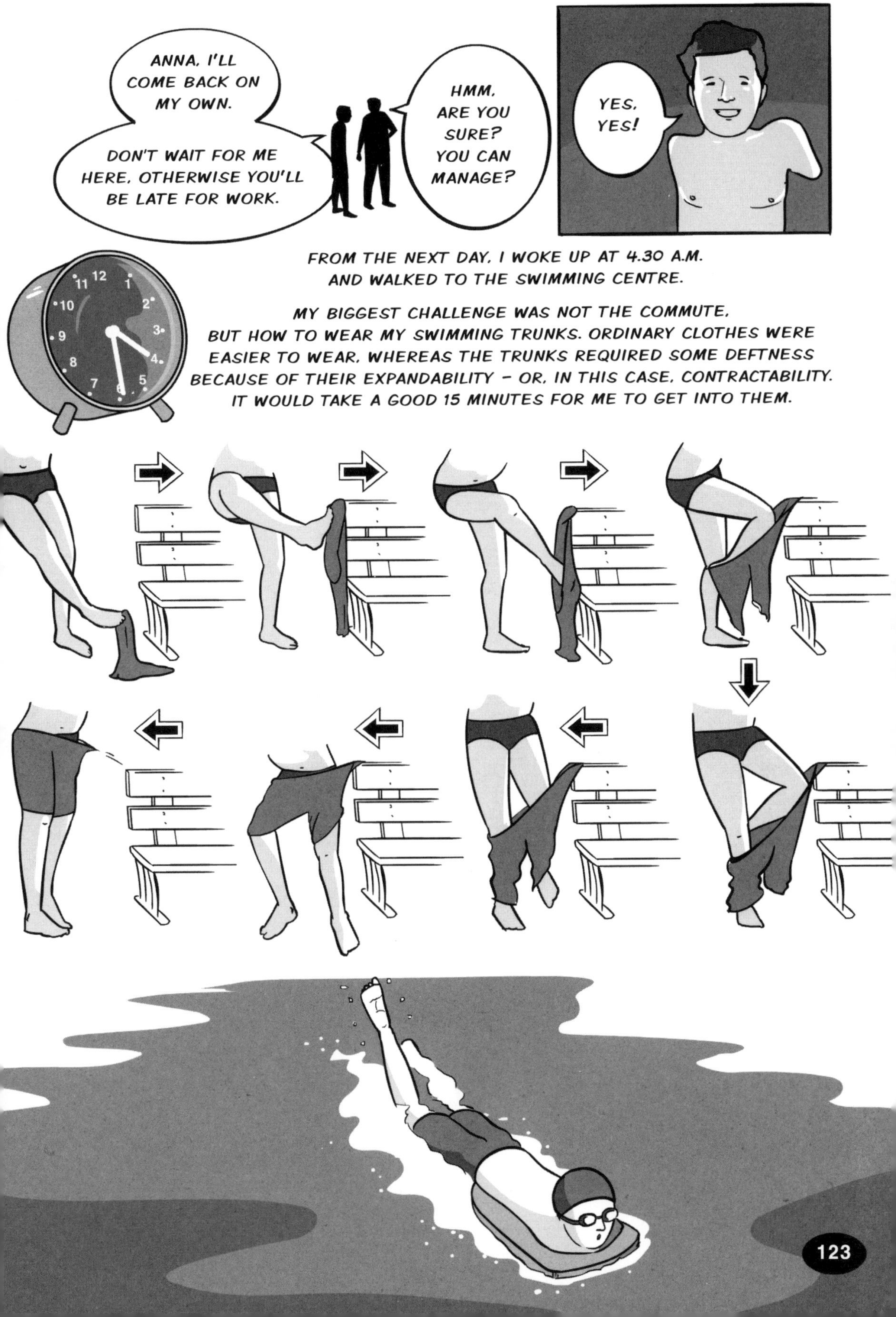
ANNA, I'LL COME BACK ON MY OWN.
DON'T WAIT FOR ME HERE, OTHERWISE YOU'LL BE LATE FOR WORK.
HMM, ARE YOU SURE? YOU CAN MANAGE?
YES, YES!
FROM THE NEXT DAY, I WOKE UP AT 4.30 A.M. AND WALKED TO THE SWIMMING CENTRE.
MY BIGGEST CHALLENGE WAS NOT THE COMMUTE, BUT HOW TO WEAR MY SWIMMING TRUNKS. ORDINARY CLOTHES WERE EASIER TO WEAR, WHEREAS THE TRUNKS REQUIRED SOME DEFTNESS BECAUSE OF THEIR EXPANDABILITY – OR, IN THIS CASE, CONTRACTABILITY. IT WOULD TAKE A GOOD 15 MINUTES FOR ME TO GET INTO THEM.

CAN YOU SWIM ON YOUR OWN NOW?
ONLY WITH ACCESSORIES. BUT I'LL GET THERE SOON.
NICE! SWIMMING, KUNG FU. WHAT'S NEXT, MY FRIEND?!
NATYALO
DANCE
COMPAN
YIKES, I'M LATE TODAY TOO!
JUST SIT HERE.
I'LL BE DONE IN AN HOUR.
OK.
OK, EVERYONE! ONE MORE TIME.
4, 3, 2, 1

FOR THE FIRST TIME, I SAW MYSELF IN A FULL-LENGTH MIRROR.
AND FOR THE FIRST TIME, I FELT POSITIVE ABOUT THE WAY I LOOKED.
WHEN I LOOKED IN THE MIRROR, I DIDN'T SEE WHAT WAS MISSING. INSTEAD, I SAW WHAT I WAS CAPABLE OF.
WHAT'S WRONG WITH THE WAY I LOOK?
WHY SHOULD I BE ASHAMED OF MY BODY?
IT'S NOT LIKE I COMMITTED A CRIME.
THIS IS JUST THE WAY I AM!
I AM NOT GOING TO HIDE ANYMORE!
IT WAS A MOMENT OF SELF-REALIZATION AND SELF-ACCEPTANCE.
IT BROUGHT ABOUT A SEA OF CHANGE IN MY CONFIDENCE.
I DECIDED TO DISCARD THE SHAWL AND THE PROSTHETIC ARMS, AND STEP INTO THE WORLD AS I WAS.

AND AT THAT MOMENT, I MADE ANOTHER DECISION.
YOU ASKED ME WHAT'S NEXT.
DANCE - THAT'S WHAT I AM GOING TO LEARN.
THUS BEGAN MY TRYST WITH DANCING.

SWIMMING CLASSES, MARTIAL ARTS, DANCE – MY DAY WAS ALMOST PACKED. I WAS SO ADDICTED TO ANY FORM OF PHYSICAL ACTIVITY THAT I WANTED TO TRY EVERYTHING THAT WAS ACCESSIBLE TO ME.

WITH A FEW HOURS STILL NOT UTILIZED ON SOME DAYS OF THE WEEK, I JOINED GYMNASTICS.

BUT THE COMMUTE WAS SO CHALLENGING THAT I HAD TO DROP OUT.

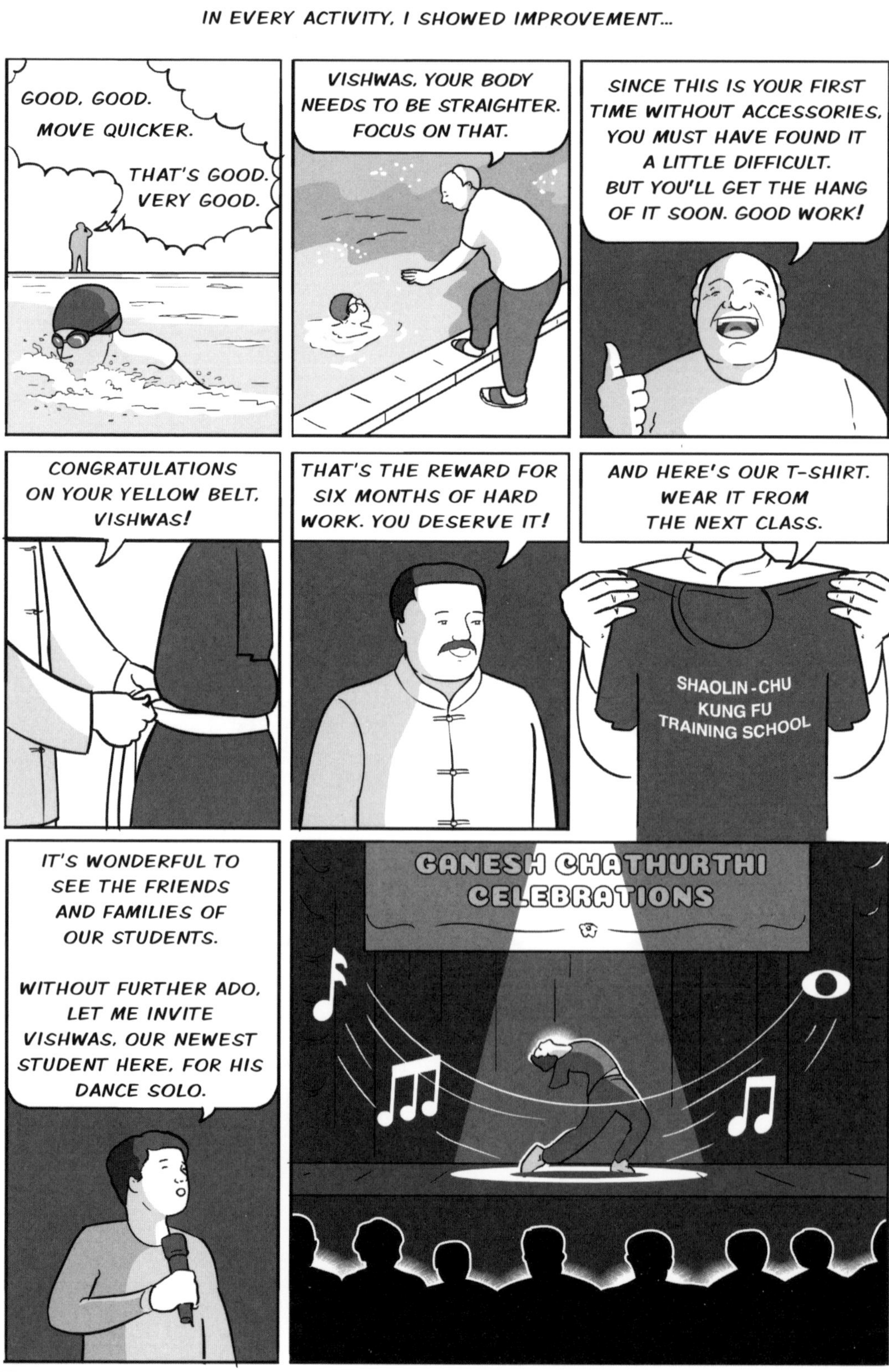

IN EVERY ACTIVITY, I SHOWED IMPROVEMENT...
GOOD, GOOD.
MOVE QUICKER.
THAT'S GOOD. VERY GOOD.
VISHWAS, YOUR BODY NEEDS TO BE STRAIGHTER. FOCUS ON THAT.
SINCE THIS IS YOUR FIRST TIME WITHOUT ACCESSORIES, YOU MUST HAVE FOUND IT A LITTLE DIFFICULT. BUT YOU'LL GET THE HANG OF IT SOON. GOOD WORK!
CONGRATULATIONS ON YOUR YELLOW BELT, VISHWAS!
THAT'S THE REWARD FOR SIX MONTHS OF HARD WORK. YOU DESERVE IT!
AND HERE'S OUR T-SHIRT. WEAR IT FROM THE NEXT CLASS.
SHAOLIN-CHU KUNG FU TRAINING SCHOOL
IT'S WONDERFUL TO SEE THE FRIENDS AND FAMILIES OF OUR STUDENTS.
WITHOUT FURTHER ADO, LET ME INVITE VISHWAS, OUR NEWEST STUDENT HERE, FOR HIS DANCE SOLO.
GANESH CHATHURTHI CELEBRATIONS

...AND I WAS READY TO MOVE TO THE NEXT LEVEL.

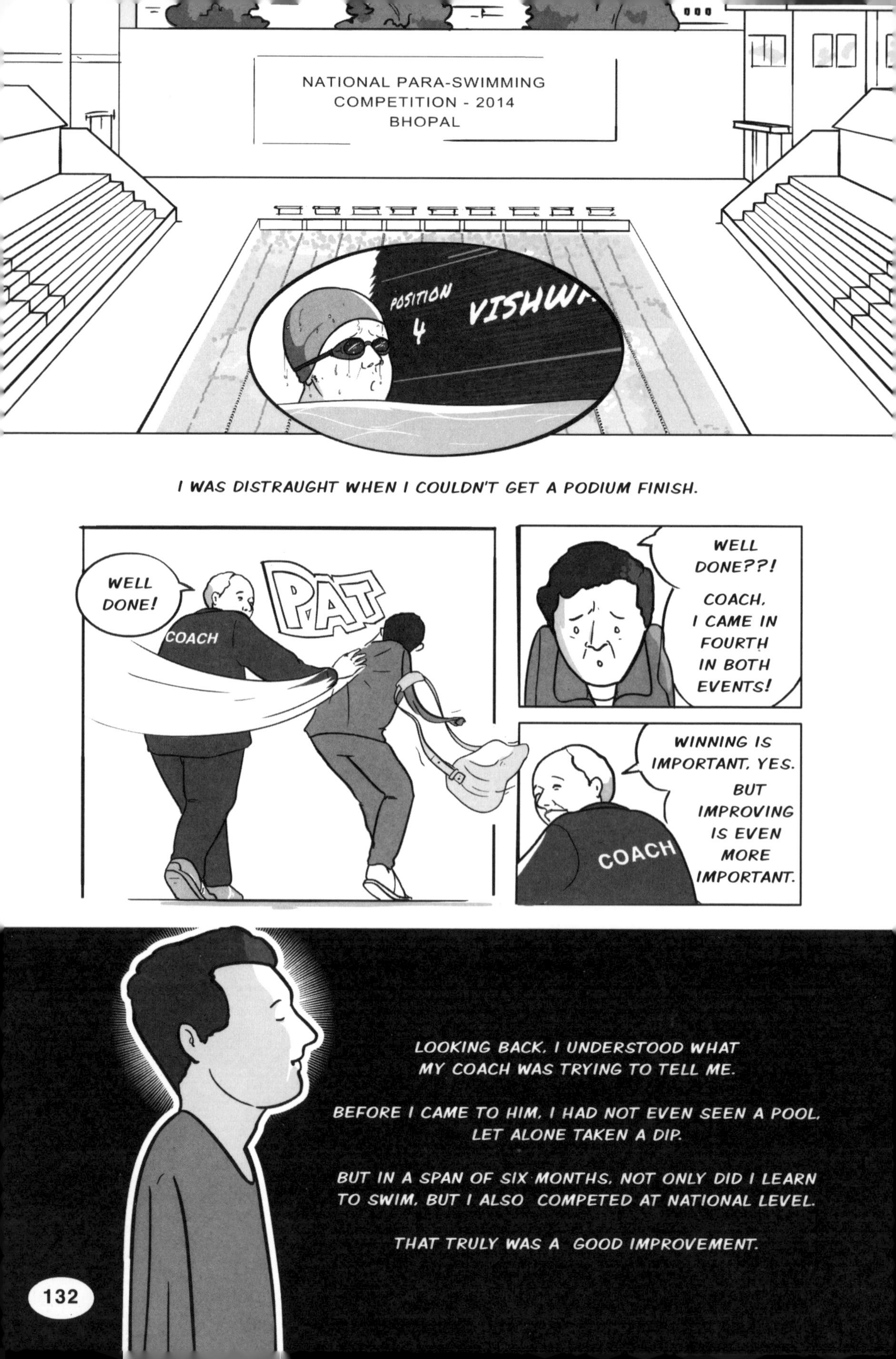
NATIONAL PARA-SWIMMING
COMPETITION - 2014
BHOPAL
POSITION
4
VISHWA
I WAS DISTRAUGHT WHEN I COULDN'T GET A PODIUM FINISH.
WELL DONE!
PAT
COACH
WELL DONE??! COACH, I CAME IN FOURTH IN BOTH EVENTS!
WINNING IS IMPORTANT, YES. BUT IMPROVING IS EVEN MORE IMPORTANT.
COACH
LOOKING BACK, I UNDERSTOOD WHAT MY COACH WAS TRYING TO TELL ME.
BEFORE I CAME TO HIM, I HAD NOT EVEN SEEN A POOL, LET ALONE TAKEN A DIP.
BUT IN A SPAN OF SIX MONTHS, NOT ONLY DID I LEARN TO SWIM, BUT I ALSO COMPETED AT NATIONAL LEVEL.
THAT TRULY WAS A GOOD IMPROVEMENT.

NOT HAVING A PODIUM FINISH ONLY MADE ME MORE DETERMINED.
I WANTED TO COMPETE MORE AND START WINNING.

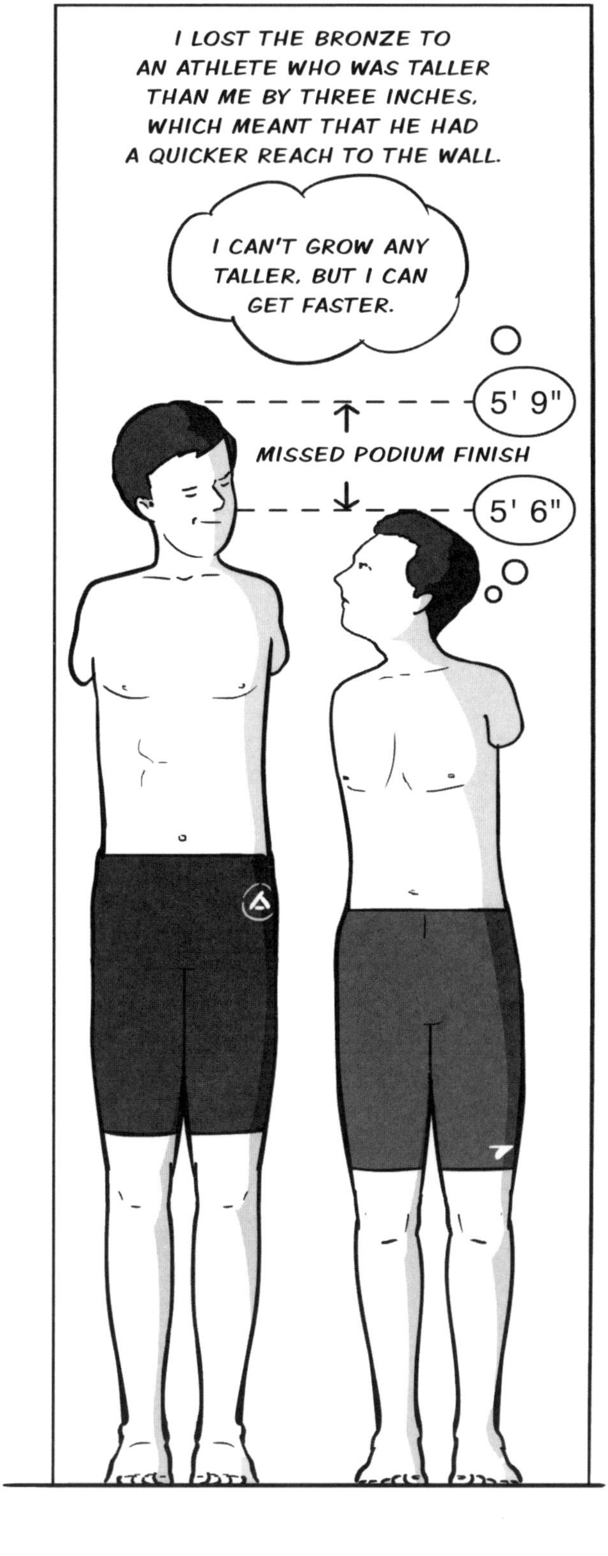

I STARTED PUTTING IN MORE EFFORT AND SPENT A LOT OF TIME IN TRAINING.

EVERY SESSION STARTED WITH WARM-UPS AND 15 LAPS EACH OF FREESTYLE AND BACKSTROKE.

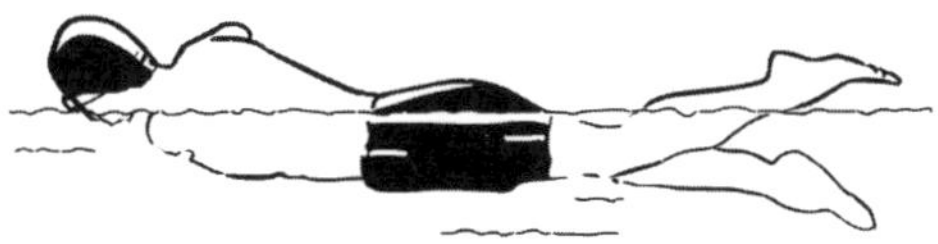

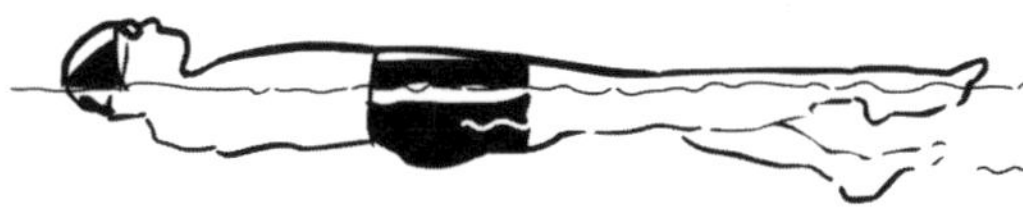

I BEGAN PRACTISING THE BREAST AND BUTTERFLY STROKES, TOO.

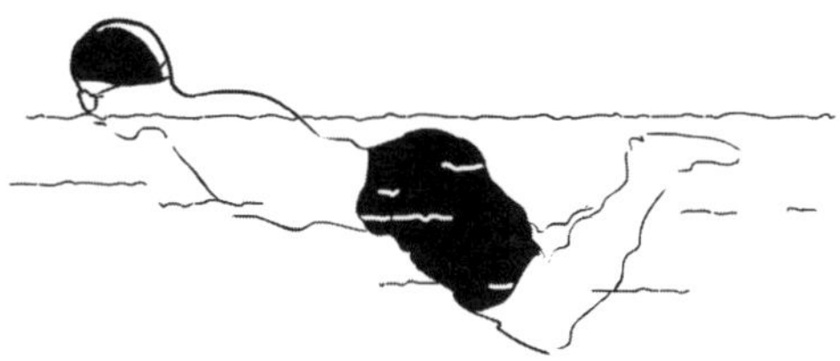

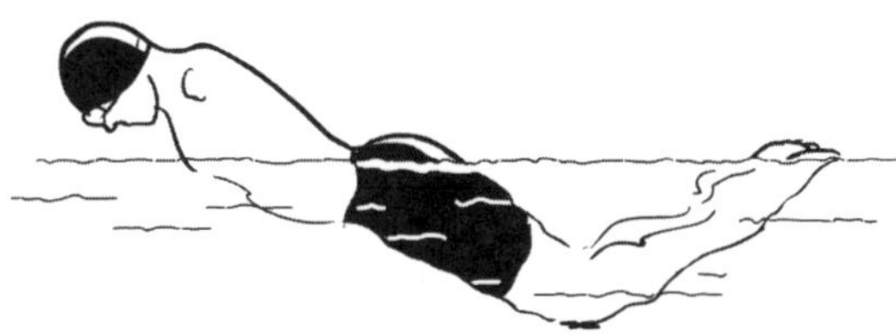

INSTANTLY, THE FLY BECAME MY FAVOURITE. SOMEHOW, I FELT THAT I WAS A NATURAL AT IT.

IF I HAD DONE 10 REPETITIONS EARLIER, I NOW DID 50 OR SOMETIMES 70 REPS. DOING THE SAME THING DAY IN AND DAY OUT DID GET BORING.
THE DIFFERENCE BETWEEN JUST TRAINING AND TRAINING TO WIN IS THAT YOU NEED TO DO THE SAME THING OVER AND OVER AGAIN, EVEN IF IT GETS BORING. YOU HAVE TO AIM FOR EFFICIENCY.
I HAD SET MY SIGHTS ON A MEDAL.
MY FOCUS WAS UNWAVERING.

STATE SWIMMING MEET KARNATAKA
STATE SWIMMING MEET KARNATAKA
STATE SWIMMING MEET KARNATAKA
MORE PRACTICE MEANT GREATER IMPROVEMENT, AND BETTER RESULTS.
WELL DONE, VISHWAS!
THANK YOU, COACH. THANK YOU FOR ALL THE TRAINING AND GUIDANCE.
YOU HAVE SPENT SO MUCH TIME ON ME. IT WOULDN'T HAVE BEEN POSSIBLE WITHOUT YOU.
ALL THE HOURS YOU HAVE SPENT ON ME – REALLY, THANK YOU, COACH.
YOU ARE GIVING A SPEECH AS THOUGH YOU ARE GOING TO RETIRE FROM SWIMMING!
NO RELAXING! YOU HAVE TO KEEP TRAINING. THERE'S NO QUITTING, EVEN IF YOU WIN GOLD!
QUIT TRAINING? THAT'S NEVER GOING TO HAPPEN!
I KNEW NOW WHAT MOMENTUM COULD DO. MORE IMPORTANTLY, I KNEW WHAT LETHARGY COULD DO, AND I WAS NOT GOING TO FALL INTO THAT PIT AGAIN.

NOT JUST IN SWIMMING, I WAS MAKING RAPID STRIDES
IN OTHER ACTIVITIES AS WELL.

DURING MY DANCE SCHOOL'S ANNUAL DAY CELEBRATION,
I WAS GIVEN THE OPPORTUNITY TO PERFORM IN FRONT OF A BIG CROWD.

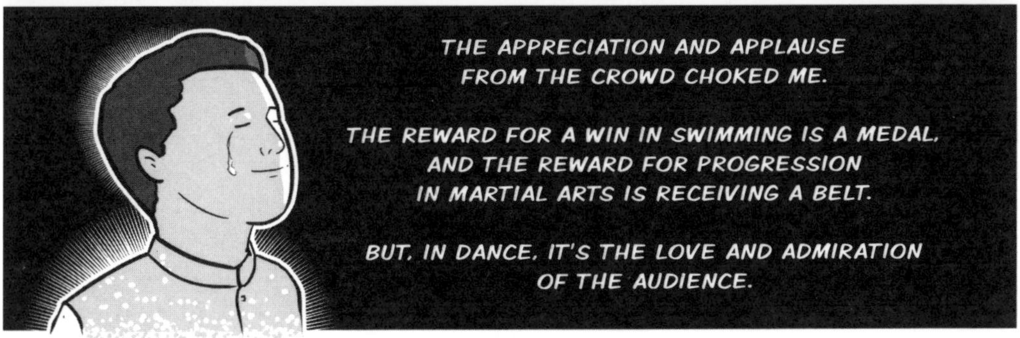

SOCIAL MEDIA HELPED ME GAIN RECOGNITION.
A VIDEO SHOT BY PEOPLE IN THE AUDIENCE WAS CIRCULATED WIDELY...

...AND I GOT NOTICED AT THE RIGHT PLACES.

GOOD EVENING. WE ARE CALLING FROM ETV, HYDERABAD.
WE SAW YOU PERFORM IN A VIDEO AND WERE VERY IMPRESSED.
WE WOULD LIKE TO HAVE YOU ON OUR DANCE PROGRAMME AS A GUEST PERFORMER.
AND THAT'S HOW I LANDED MY FIRST OFFER FOR A PERFORMANCE ON A TV SHOW.

THAT WAS BRILLIANT, VISHWAS! IT WAS A MIND-BLOWING PERFORMANCE!
THANK YOU, MADAM.

TOP CLASS! WHEN I SEE YOU - IT'S NOT SYMPATHY, JUST PRIDE. YOUR ATTITUDE AND YOUR POSITIVITY JUST OOZES OUT.
MA'AM, VISHWAS IS ALSO A MARTIAL ARTIST AND SWIMMER.
REALLY? THAT'S AMAZING! TELL US ABOUT YOURSELF, YOUR LIFE.
I LOST MY ARMS WHEN I WAS 10...
...MY FATHER DIED TRYING TO SAVE ME...
...MY MOTHER DIED A FEW YEARS AGO...
...NOBODY WAS WILLING TO EMPLOY ME...
...I JOINED KUNG FU, NOW I HAVE A BLUE BELT...
...I HAD TIME, SO I LEARNED SWIMMING...
...WON MEDALS AT THE STATE MEET...
...STARTED TRAINING IN DANCE AS WELL.
I'M IN AWE! REALLY!
SO MANY OF US, SO-CALLED ABLED PEOPLE, LAZE AROUND AND WASTE TIME.
WHEREAS, YOU HAVE UTILIZED YOUR TIME TO THE FULLEST.
YOU HAVE SHOWN THAT DISABILITY IS ONLY IN ONE'S MIND.
ABSOLUTELY RIGHT ABOUT THAT.
YOU ARE SUCH AN INSPIRATION, VISHWAS!
YOUR PERFORMANCE WAS JUST MAGNIFICENT!
IT FILLED ME WITH SO MUCH HAPPINESS!
YES, YOUR MOVES ARE VERY REFINED AND THIS FLEXIBILITY CAN BE ACHIEVED ONLY THROUGH YEARS OF PRACTICE.
YOU MUST HAVE TRAINED REALLY HARD TO ACCOMPLISH ALL THIS IN SUCH A SHORT PERIOD OF TIME. REALLY GOOD!

THANK YOU, SIR.
I JUST WANT TO MAKE A REQUEST TO ALL YOU JUDGES.
SURE, VISHWAS, GO AHEAD.
IF WE HAVE THE TIME NOW, CAN I PERFORM A SOLO DANCE?
WITH PLEASURE, VISHWAS! WE WILL MAKE TIME FOR YOU.
VISHWAS, MARVELLOUS! PLEASE COME AND SIT WITH US. GIVE US THE PLEASURE OF WATCHING THE REST OF THE SHOW WITH YOU.
THAT SHOW PUT ME ON THE RADAR OF TV NETWORKS.

I WAS ESPECIALLY THRILLED WHEN I WAS INVITED TO DANCE FOR A KANNADA CHANNEL.

LIKE I WAS GOING TO MISS THAT! HOW OFTEN DOES ONE GET AN OPPORTUNITY TO PERFORM IN FRONT OF ONE'S FAVOURITE MOVIE STAR!

I DANCED TO A MEDLEY OF SONGS FROM UPENDRA'S MOVIES. SAFE TO SAY, I HAD DONE ENOUGH TO IMPRESS HIM.
MAJAA TALKIES WAS POPULAR, UPENDRA WAS POPULAR. SO...

...I BECAME POPULAR AS WELL.

WITH NEARLY ALL OF BANGALORE WATCHING THAT SHOW, THERE WAS NO WAY I WAS NOT GOING TO GET NOTICED.

EARLIER, PEOPLE LOOKED AT ME FOR WHAT I LACKED. BUT NOW, THEY WERE LOOKING AT WHAT I COULD DO.

IF MY FIRST TV SHOW PUT ME ON THE MAP OF TELEVISION NETWORKS, THIS SHOW WAS THE SPRINGBOARD TO MY CAREER IN DANCE.

I BEGAN TO ACCEPT EVERY INVITATION.

AND THE MORE I PERFORMED, THE MORE I WAS NOTICED.
...ANNUAL DAY...
...ON THE 31ST...
...AND WE'LL PAY RS 500 FOR YOUR PERFORMANCE.
OH. THAT'S NICE OF THEM!
THIS I THOUGHT WAS A ONE-OFF, UNTIL I STARTED RECEIVING MORE SUCH OFFERS.
...RS 1000...
WE'LL SEND A CAR TO PICK YOU UP AND THEN DROP YOU, AS WELL.
...RS 750...
...RS 1250...
THAT'S WHEN IT OCCURRED TO ME THAT I COULD MAKE A LIVING AS A DANCER.
WITH MORE PERFORMANCES, CAME MORE MONEY.

BUT, IT ALSO HAD ITS DRAWBACKS.

I WAS BEGINNING TO SEE A CONSISTENT INFLOW OF MONEY FROM MY DANCE PERFORMANCES.

EARNINGS, WHICH I HAD NEVER HAD TILL THAT POINT.

MY OWN MONEY, WHICH I COULD SPEND ON WHATEVER I NEEDED.

ಕರ್ನಾಟಕ ಸರ್ಕಾರ

THE REWARD MOTIVATED ME FURTHER.
I CAME TO BELIEVE THAT ONLY HARD WORK CAN BRING SUCCESS.
I WORKED HARDER, PRACTISED MORE...
...AND GOT MORE TIRED.
AT ONE POINT, I WAS RUNNING ON MENTAL STRENGTH RATHER THAN PHYSICAL STRENGTH.
TRRiiiNG TRRiiiNG

HELLO, VISHWAS.
WE ARE CALLING FROM THE SWIMMING FEDERATION OF INDIA. CONGRATULATIONS! YOU HAVE BEEN SELECTED TO PARTICIPATE IN AN INTERNATIONAL MEET IN CANADA.
YOU HAVE THREE-FOUR MONTHS TO TRAIN.
YOUR TIMING IN BELGAUM WAS GOOD ENOUGH FOR THIS QUALIFICATION. THE EVENT IS IN JULY.
WE'LL MAKE THE ARRANGEMENTS FOR YOUR FLIGHT AND ACCOMMODATION. FOR THE VISA, YOU'LL HAVE TO PAY RS 80,000.
WE'LL NEED A COPY OF YOUR BANK STATEMENT, AND YOU'LL NEED TO HAVE AT LEAST TWO LAKHS IN THE ACCOUNT.
WE'LL GET IN TOUCH WITH MORE DETAILS.
TRAIN HARD, AND DON'T WASTE TIME. IT'S NOT AN OPPORTUNITY THAT EVERYONE GETS. MAKE THE MOST OF IT. ALL THE BEST!
OK. TH...THANK YOU.
CLICK
WHAT WAS THAT?
AN INTERNATIONAL EVENT?
BUT RS 80,000! TWO LAKHS! WHERE WILL I GO FOR THAT KIND OF MONEY? HOW CAN I ARRANGE IT?
BUT, WHAT AN OPPORTUNITY?! CANADA!!!
IS THIS EVEN REAL?? WHAT IF IT'S A FAKE CALL??
YES, THAT MUST BE IT. SOME PRANKSTER OR FRAUDSTER AFTER MY MONEY!
BUT, WHAT IF IT IS REAL?
OHH, THAT WOULD BE...
ARRGHH, NO NO. IT CAN'T BE...
...BUT, WHAT IF IT IS? WHAT IF IT IS TRUE?

FORTUNATELY FOR ME, IT TURNED OUT TO BE AUTHENTIC.

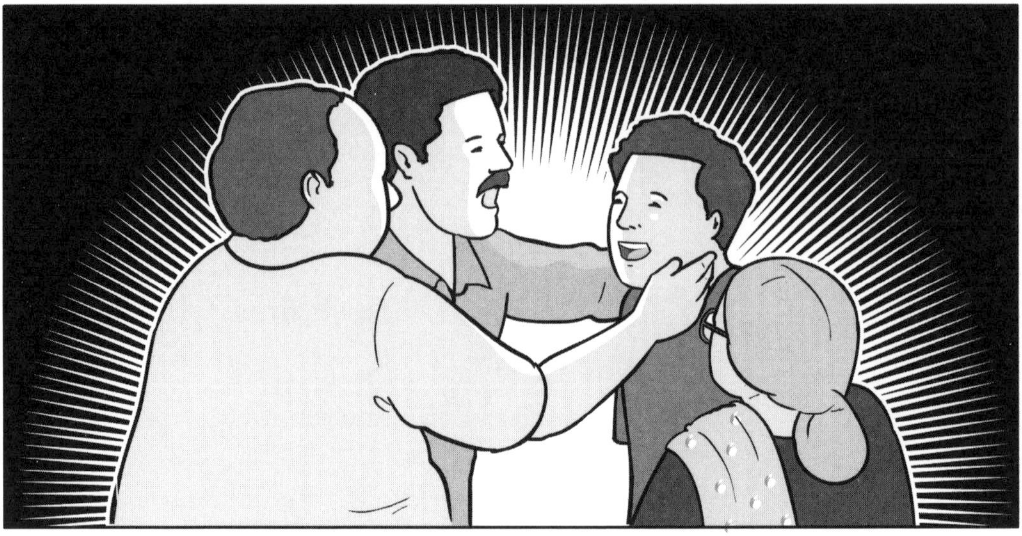

IT CERTAINLY WAS A GREAT OPPORTUNITY,
BUT IT WOULD HAPPEN ONLY IF I COULD FIND THE MONEY FOR IT.

NOT THAT I WAS A PESSIMIST, BUT THERE WERE OTHER THINGS
THAT I WAS WORRIED ABOUT WHICH WOULD COST A LOT.

THIS WAS AN INTERNATIONAL EVENT. SO I HAD TO BE IN TOP CONDITION TO COMPETE – MY FITNESS, MY DIET, EVERYTHING NEEDED TO BE SPOT ON. MOST IMPORTANTLY, MY TRAINING HAD TO BE SPECIAL, TAILORED TO MY NEEDS.

WITH THAT TAKEN CARE OF, I HAD ONE MORE THING TO SORT OUT - MONEY.

THEY SAY, WHEN YOU PUT YOUR HONEST EFFORT INTO WHAT YOU WANT TO DO, THE UNIVERSE WILL BRING EVERYTHING NECESSARY FOR YOU TO ACCOMPLISH THE TASK.

IT CERTAINLY DID FOR ME.
I FOUND A BACKER - BOOKMYSHOW.

I WAS RELIEVED. BECAUSE I DIDN'T WANT TO BURDEN MY FAMILY WITH THIS.

MY SINCERITY AND EARNESTNESS HAVE BEEN MY BUILDING BLOCKS THROUGHOUT LIFE. I'M PROUD OF MYSELF FOR HAVING SUSTAINED THESE VALUES.

FOR EVERY DANCE PERFORMANCE, I LEARNED A NEW NUMBER. I WANTED TO REPAY THE TRUST THAT PEOPLE HAD SHOWN IN ME. THIS WAS NO DIFFERENT. MY BENEFACTOR HAD PUT ENORMOUS FAITH IN ME. I WAS NOT GOING TO LET THEM DOWN - IF NOT RESULT-WISE, AT LEAST EFFORT-WISE.

I DOUBLED MY EFFORTS, DOUBLED MY TRAINING AND DOUBLED MY FOCUS.

I REDUCED MY TRAINING IN MARTIAL ARTS AND DANCE. BUT I ACCEPTED ONE OR TWO INVITATIONS TO DANCE SHOWS, ESPECIALLY IF IT WAS FOR TV.

AFTER THREE MONTHS OF INTENSE AND RIGOROUS TRAINING,
I WAS BRIMMING WITH CONFIDENCE AND WAS READY TO TAKE ON NEW CHALLENGES.

MY FIRST FLIGHT EXPERIENCE WAS AWESOME!

AND I WAS FASCINATED BY THE ELEGANT BEAUTY OF THE ARENA.

BUT WHAT WAS EVEN MORE IMPRESSIVE WAS HOW WELL-BUILT THE SWIMMERS FROM OTHER COUNTRIES WERE.
ARTISTS WOULD HAVE FOUND INSPIRATION HERE.
WE ARE GOING TO COMPETE AGAINST SWIMMERS LIKE THEM?!
INDIA
HA. HA. YES, MY FRIEND.
INDIA
THEY LOOK MASSIVE! SO WELL BUILT! IT LOOKS AS THOUGH THEY SPEND ALL THEIR TIME IN THE GYM!
YES, THEY DO WORKOUT A LOT.
THEY USUALLY HAVE LONG-TERM SPONSORS TO SUPPORT THEM FOR SIX OR SEVEN YEARS. THAT WAY, THESE SWIMMERS DON'T HAVE TO BOTHER ABOUT EARNING TO SUPPORT THEIR TRAINING. IT'S DISTRACTION-FREE.
TRAINING, DIET, PHYSIO – EVERYTHING'S TAKEN CARE OF.
WOW, THAT EXPLAINS IT.
I BET THEY ARE SUPER FAST AS WELL!

ALRIGHT, ALRIGHT, DON'T GET DISTRACTED NOW. GATHER AROUND.
INDIA
INDIA
REMEMBER THAT YOU ARE ALL HERE BECAUSE YOU DESERVE TO BE HERE. YOU HAVE QUALIFIED BASED ON YOUR TIMINGS, WHICH WERE GOOD ENOUGH TO COMPETE WITH THESE ATHLETES.
INDIA MANAGER
INDIA
YOU DON'T KNOW IF THEIR QUALIFYING TIME WAS BETTER OR WORSE THAN YOURS, SO DON'T THINK ABOUT ALL THAT. JUST FOCUS ON YOURSELF.
AND REMEMBER THAT YOU HAVE TRAINED HARD.
INDEED, WE HAD ALL TRAINED WELL. EACH ONE OF US HAD PUT OUR HEART AND SOUL INTO PREPARING FOR THIS.
WEEKS AND WEEKS OF TRAINING FOR AN EVENT THAT WOULD LAST ONLY A FEW SECONDS - THOSE FEW SECONDS WHICH WOULD GIVE US AN OPPORTUNITY TO BRING GLORY TO OUR COUNTRY.
I WAS READY. THAT DIP IN MY CONFIDENCE WAS, WELL, MOMENTARY. IT WAS NOW TIME TO SET ASIDE ANY DOUBTS AND GIVE MY BEST.

HEATS

FINAL

NO WORDS COULD DESCRIBE MY JOY.
THIS WAS MY BIT FOR MY COUNTRY.
NEWS OF MY ACHIEVEMENT BEGAN TO SPREAD EVEN BEFORE I ARRIVED HOME.
2 SILVER, 1 BRONZE
Vishwas KS Wins Big
PARASWIMMER FROM BENGALURU
WINS BIG IN CANADA
2 Silver, 1 Bronze for Vishwas at Can AmPara Swimming Competition
MEDAL TALLY
CANADA GLORY
FOR BENGALURU PARASWIMMER
ALTHOUGH THE COVERAGE WAS NOT AS BIG AS IT WAS FOR OTHER POPULAR SPORTS, IT DID RESULT IN OTHER THINGS.
KEMPEGOWDA AWARD
KARNATAKA
ETV
VISHWAS KS PARASWIMMER
WINNER CANADA
entral government has cut excise duty on oil, diesel, petroleum products imported
విశ్వాస్
AND MOST IMPORTANTLY, BOOKMYSHOW AGREED TO EXTEND THEIR SUPPORT FOR ANOTHER TWO YEARS!
THAT WAS A SIGNIFICANT MOMENT.
BECAUSE I WAS NOW BEING RECOGNIZED AS A TOP ATHLETE - AN ATHLETE WHO HAD THE POTENTIAL TO QUALIFY FOR THE 2018 ASIAN GAMES!

THE MERE MENTION OF THE ASIAN GAMES WAS ENOUGH FOR ME TO TAKE MY EFFORTS TO A WHOLE NEW LEVEL.

I MOVED INTO A PG ACCOMMODATION CLOSER TO MY SWIMMING COACHING CENTRE.

IT WAS ONE OF THE WISEST DECISIONS I EVER MADE.

BY NOT HAVING TO COMMUTE ACROSS THE CITY, I SAVED A LOT OF TIME, AND ENERGY, WHICH I THEN INVESTED IN TRAINING.

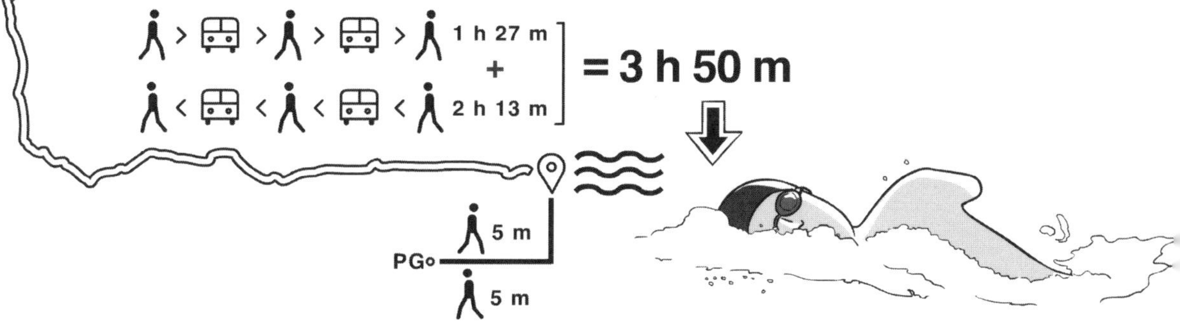

WHATEVER I COULD GIVE UP TO EARN MORE TIME, I DID, WHICH INCLUDED STAYING AWAY FROM MY PHONE. I ALLOTTED A SPECIFIC TIME FOR THAT.

MY DAY WAS PACKED, AND IT LOOKED MORE OR LESS LIKE THIS -

THIS SCHEDULE WOULD CONTINUE FOR THE NEXT TWO YEARS WITH THE AIM OF COMPETING IN THE ASIAN GAMES IN 2018.

BUT WHEN IT CAME TO TV SHOWS, I ACCEPTED THE OFFER WITHOUT HESITATION.

WHAT CONTACTS? WHAT CAN YOU GET?
THESE TV SHOWS - ALL THEY ARE LOOKING FOR IS TO INCREASE THEIR TRP RATINGS.
THAT'S WHY THEY KEEP ASKING YOU ABOUT YOUR STORY. AS IF THEY DON'T KNOW IT ALREADY!
THEY MAKE YOU NARRATE YOUR STORY AND ADD A BACKGROUND SCORE, MAKING IT INTO A BIG DRAMA.
THAT'S THE WAY IT IS, MANJU.
I DON'T LIKE IT, BUT I'VE ACCEPTED IT.
EVEN THE SMALLER STAGE EVENTS GIVE YOU SOME MONEY WHEN THEY DON'T HAVE MUCH THEMSELVES!
WELL, AT LEAST THEY CAN PAY YOU!
TV MAKES ENORMOUS MONEY. CAN'T THEY GIVE YOU SOMETHING?
AS A FRIEND, I SINCERELY ADVISE YOU NOT TO GO TO THESE TV SHOWS.
LOOK, SWIMMING IS NOT A CAREER OPTION FOR ME. AT LEAST NOT LONG TERM.
MOST ATHLETES CAN GO ON UP TO THE AGE OF 38, 39 OR EVEN 40, IN SOME CASES.
WHEREAS, I CAN CONTINUE DANCING FOR A LONGER PERIOD. SO, FOR ME, THESE SHOWS ARE AN INVESTMENT. PEOPLE WILL NOTICE WHAT I CAN DO AND HOPEFULLY KEEP INVITING ME.
SPEAKING OF WHICH, I HAVE ONE SPECIAL SHOW COMING UP.

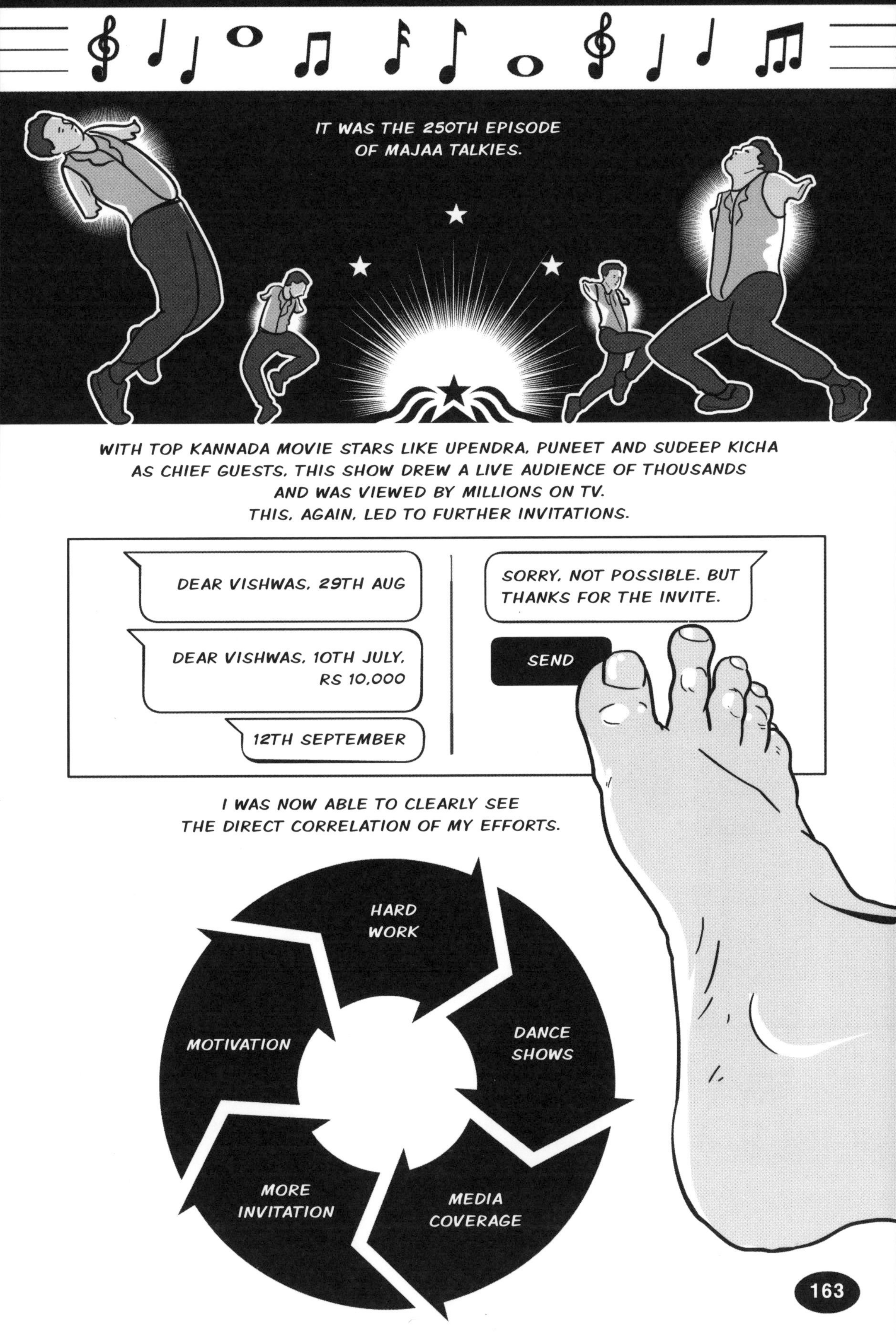
IT WAS THE 250TH EPISODE OF MAJAA TALKIES.
WITH TOP KANNADA MOVIE STARS LIKE UPENDRA, PUNEET AND SUDEEP KICHA AS CHIEF GUESTS, THIS SHOW DREW A LIVE AUDIENCE OF THOUSANDS AND WAS VIEWED BY MILLIONS ON TV. THIS, AGAIN, LED TO FURTHER INVITATIONS.
DEAR VISHWAS, 29TH AUG
DEAR VISHWAS, 10TH JULY, RS 10,000
12TH SEPTEMBER
SORRY, NOT POSSIBLE. BUT THANKS FOR THE INVITE.
SEND
I WAS NOW ABLE TO CLEARLY SEE THE DIRECT CORRELATION OF MY EFFORTS.
HARD WORK
DANCE SHOWS
MEDIA COVERAGE
MORE INVITATION
MOTIVATION

AS IT GOT CLOSER TO THE ASIAN GAMES QUALIFIERS, I STOPPED DANCE AND MARTIAL ARTS COMPLETELY TO FOCUS ONLY ON SWIMMING.
I TOOK PART IN EVERY COMPETITION THAT WAS ACCESSIBLE TO ME, AND HAD A PODIUM FINISH IN EACH OF THEM.
I WAS ON A ROLL AND MY CONFIDENCE GREW WITH EVERY MEDAL I EARNED.
WITH THAT FORM, QUALIFYING FOR THE ASIAN GAMES DIDN'T SEEM FAR-FETCHED.
A GOOD RESULT IN THE NEXT COMPETITION, THE ONE THAT MATTERED THE MOST, WOULD TAKE ME TO THE GAMES.

NATIONAL PARASWIMMING CHAMPIONSHIP BENGALURU

AND -

I HAD EXCEEDED MY OWN EXPECTATIONS.

FOUR GOLDS IN ANY EVENT IS GOOD. IT'S THE MARK OF A GOOD ATHLETE.

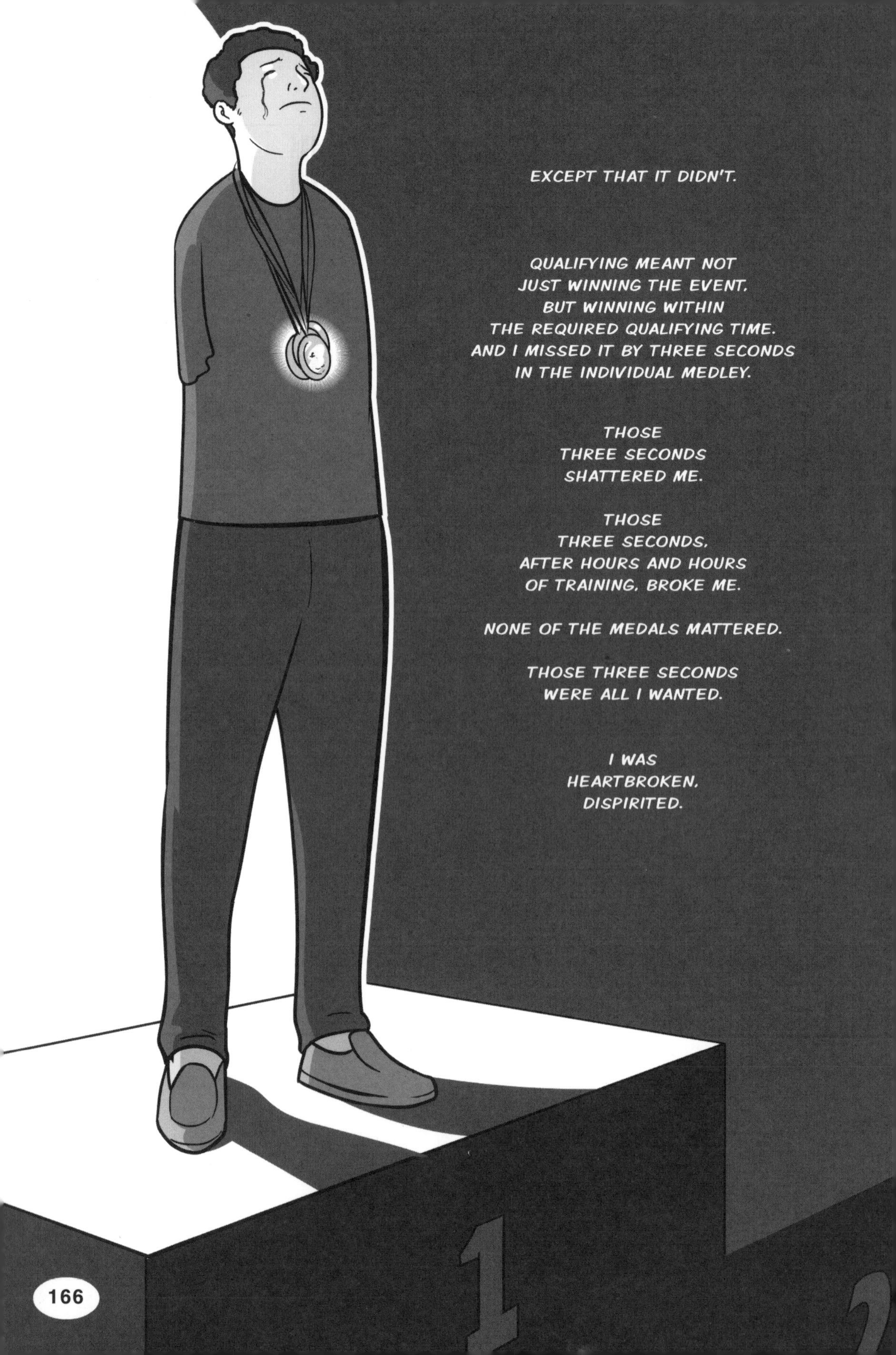
EXCEPT THAT IT DIDN'T.
QUALIFYING MEANT NOT JUST WINNING THE EVENT, BUT WINNING WITHIN THE REQUIRED QUALIFYING TIME. AND I MISSED IT BY THREE SECONDS IN THE INDIVIDUAL MEDLEY.
THOSE THREE SECONDS SHATTERED ME.
THOSE THREE SECONDS, AFTER HOURS AND HOURS OF TRAINING, BROKE ME.
NONE OF THE MEDALS MATTERED.
THOSE THREE SECONDS WERE ALL I WANTED.
I WAS HEARTBROKEN, DISPIRITED.

IT WAS WORSE WHEN MY PEERS RETURNED FROM THE ASIAN GAMES WITH MEDALS.

NOT THAT I WAS ENVIOUS, CERTAINLY NOT. I JUST FELT TERRIBLE TO HAVE MISSED AN OPPORTUNITY TO REPRESENT THE COUNTRY AT SUCH A BIG EVENT.

DOUBTS AND QUESTIONS CREPT INTO MY MIND.

VISHWAS, FOCUS!!
COME ON! WHAT'S THIS? IT'S BEEN DAYS NOW AND YOU ARE STILL SWIMMING AIMLESSLY. LOOK AT THIS TIMING!
SORRY, COACH.
YOU CAN'T BE LIKE THIS.
YOU NEED TO FOCUS ON THE NEXT EVENTS.
THERE ARE MORE TO COME.
YOU'VE GOT TO KEEP TRAINING, NO MATTER WHAT.
WHAT WAS THERE TO TRAIN FOR? FOR TWO YEARS, I HAD HAD A GOAL, BUT NOW, I DIDN'T HAVE ANY.
COACH, I WAS THINKING, SHALL I DO THE ENGLISH CHANNEL SWIM?
FOR WHAT?

THE RESULT OF NOT QUALIFYING FOR THE GAMES WAS THAT MY SPONSORSHIP HAD NOT BEEN EXTENDED A SECOND TIME. IT WAS ANOTHER BLOW TO MY ALREADY LOW MORALE.

TO CONTINUE TRAINING THE WAY I DID, I STARTED USING WHATEVER LITTLE SAVINGS I HAD.

HELP CAME IN A VERY UNIQUE FORM.

Accessible India Campaign

भारत सरकार
GOVERNMENT OF INDIA

सामाजिक न्याय और अधिकारिता मंत्रालय
MINISTRY OF SOCIAL JUSTICE AND EMPOWERMENT

दिव्यांगजन सशक्तिकरण विभाग
DEPARTMENT OF EMPOWERMENT OF PERSONS WITH DISABILITIES (DIVYANGJAN)

दिव्यांगजन सशक्तिकरण हेतु राष्ट्रीय पुरस्कार - 2018
NATIONAL AWARD FOR THE EMPOWERMENT OF PERSONS WITH DISABILITIES (DIVYANGJAN) - 2018

यह राष्ट्रीय पुरस्कार

श्री विश्वास के.एस.

को गतिविषयक दिव्यांगता की श्रेणी में दिव्यांगजनों के प्रेरणा स्रोत के रूप में उनके उत्कृष्ट कार्य के लिए सम्मानित करने हेतू प्रदान किया जाता है।

THIS NATIONAL AWARD IS GIVEN TO

Sh. Vishwas K. S.

IN RECOGNITION OF HIS / HER OUTSTANDING PERFORMANCE AS ROLE MODEL AMONG PERSONS WITH DISABILITIES (DIVYANGJAN) IN THE CATEGORY OF LOCOMOTOR DISABILITY

नई दिल्ली
New Delhi

दिनांक
Date 3.12.2018

सचिव, भारत सरकार
Secretary to the Government of India

THAT AWARD PUT ME ON THE MEDIA'S RADAR AGAIN.

NEWSPAPERS AND MAGAZINES WROTE ABOUT ME. TV NETWORKS INTERVIEWED ME.

SWIMMER, DANCER, MARTIAL ARTIST
NATIONAL AWARD WINNER

NATIONAL AWARD FOR PARASWIMMER
Dancer and Martial Artist, Vishwas KS

PARASWIMMING CHAMPION RECEIVES NATIONAL AWARD

I WAS VISIBLE TO THE WORLD. AGAIN.
IMMEDIATELY, I STARTED RECEIVING REQUESTS TO PERFORM AT VARIOUS PLACES.

I WAS RECEIVING MORE OPPORTUNITIES THAN EVER.
THIS TIME, I ACCEPTED EVERY ONE OF THEM.

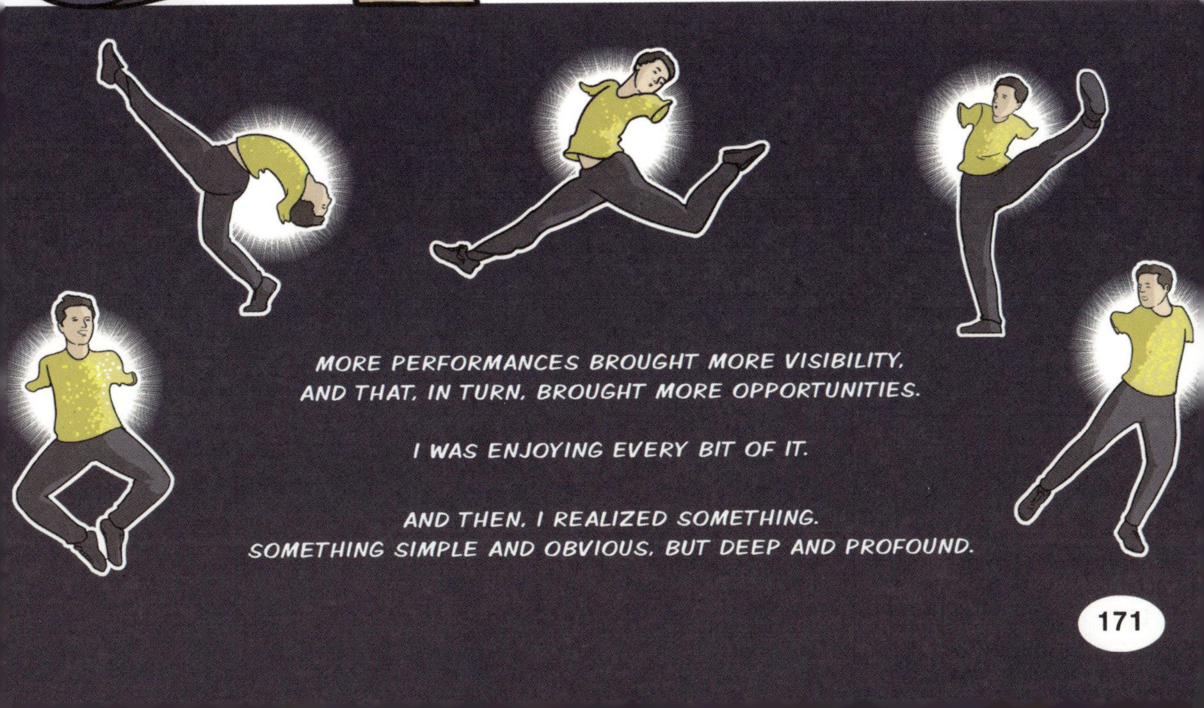

HARD WORK ALWAYS PAYS OFF.
IT MAY NOT BRING THE OUTCOME I DESIRE, BUT IT WILL ALWAYS RESULT IN SOMETHING GOOD. MAYBE NOT TODAY, OR NOT EVEN TOMORROW, BUT IT'LL HAPPEN SOMEDAY. IF NOTHING, I'LL AT LEAST HAVE THE SATISFACTION OF DOING MY BEST. AFTER ALL, BEING EARNEST AND SINCERE ARE THE ONLY THINGS THAT MATTER THE MOST.
THAT REALIZATION BROUGHT OUT A NEW VIGOUR IN ME. IT BROUGHT A SENSE OF PURPOSE.
I WAS IN A BETTER HEADSPACE. I WAS ABLE TO FOCUS ON MY TRAINING AGAIN.
WORLD CHAMPIONSHIPS...
...HERE I COME!
SPLASH
SHOWS AND TRAINING KEPT ME ON MY TOES.
FOR SOME SHOWS, I HAD TO TRAVEL TO FAR-OFF PLACES AND GET BACK PAST MIDNIGHT, AND WAKE UP THE NEXT MORNING FOR TRAINING. IT WAS EXHAUSTING. BUT I WAS WILLING TO PUT IN THE HOURS AS I NEEDED THE MONEY TO CONTINUE MY TRAINING.

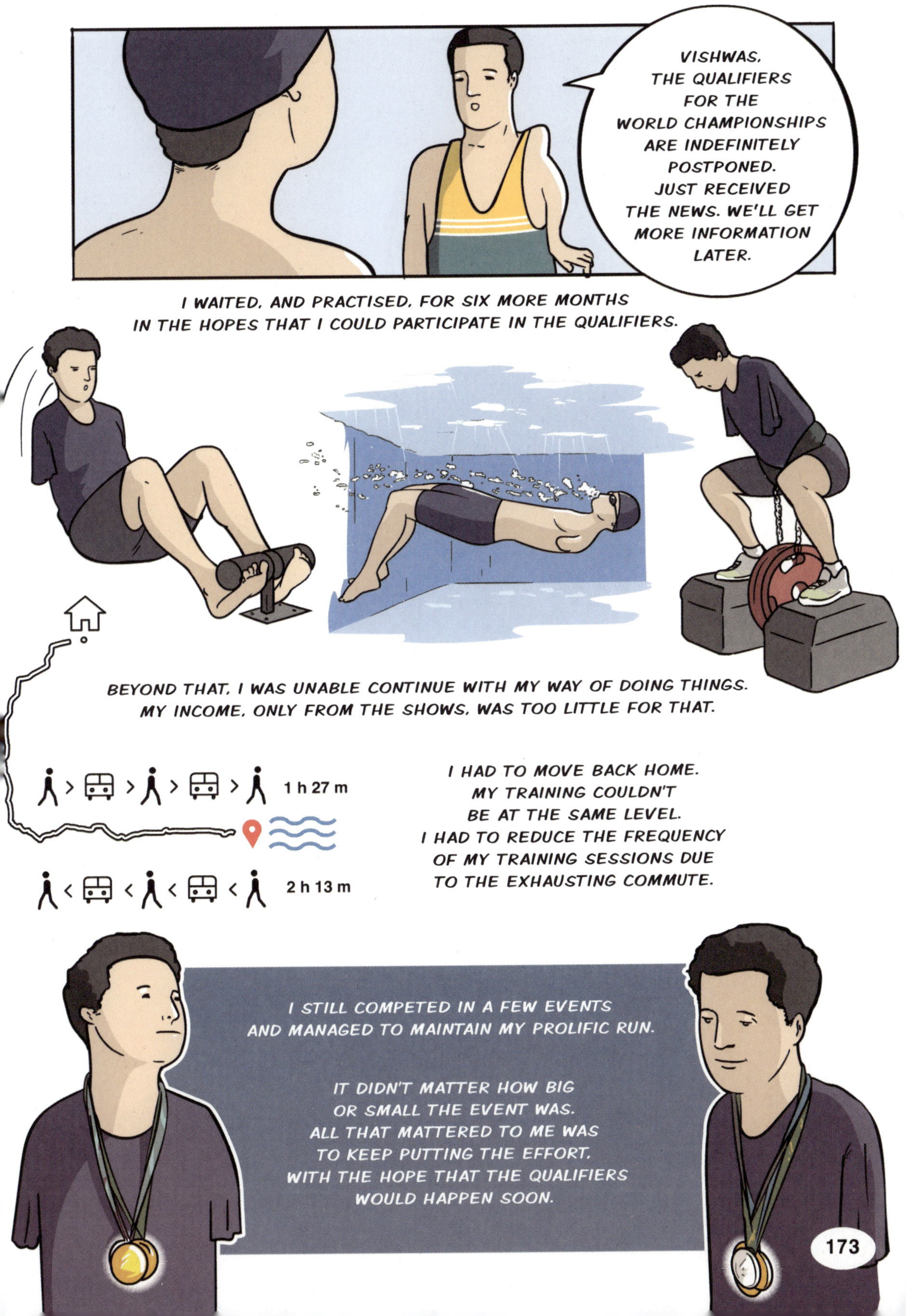
VISHWAS, THE QUALIFIERS FOR THE WORLD CHAMPIONSHIPS ARE INDEFINITELY POSTPONED. JUST RECEIVED THE NEWS. WE'LL GET MORE INFORMATION LATER.
I WAITED, AND PRACTISED, FOR SIX MORE MONTHS IN THE HOPES THAT I COULD PARTICIPATE IN THE QUALIFIERS.
BEYOND THAT, I WAS UNABLE CONTINUE WITH MY WAY OF DOING THINGS. MY INCOME, ONLY FROM THE SHOWS, WAS TOO LITTLE FOR THAT.
1 h 27 m
2 h 13 m
I HAD TO MOVE BACK HOME. MY TRAINING COULDN'T BE AT THE SAME LEVEL. I HAD TO REDUCE THE FREQUENCY OF MY TRAINING SESSIONS DUE TO THE EXHAUSTING COMMUTE.
I STILL COMPETED IN A FEW EVENTS AND MANAGED TO MAINTAIN MY PROLIFIC RUN.
IT DIDN'T MATTER HOW BIG OR SMALL THE EVENT WAS. ALL THAT MATTERED TO ME WAS TO KEEP PUTTING THE EFFORT, WITH THE HOPE THAT THE QUALIFIERS WOULD HAPPEN SOON.

WITH AN ALTERED TRAINING ROUTINE, I WAS ABLE TO SPEND MORE TIME ON DANCE.
TELL US A BIT ABOUT YOURSELF.
...BORN IN KOLAR...
...LOST MY ARMS...
...FATHER DIED WHILE TRYING TO SAVE ME...
...MOTHER WAS MY BACKBONE...
...SWIMMING, KUNG FU, DANCE...
...INTERNATIONAL MEDALS...
WHILE THE LIVE SHOWS BROUGHT IN MONEY, TV SHOWS BROUGHT IN A DIFFERENT TYPE OF REWARD.
WE'LL BE HONOURED, SIR, IF YOU CAN COME AS A SPEAKER TO OUR SCHOOL AT OUR ANNUAL DAY FUNCTION.
OH, THAT'S NEW!
BUT EXCITING!

NOT JUST SCHOOLS, I WAS EVEN INVITED TO SPEAK AT COLLEGES, AND SOME VERY PRESTIGIOUS EVENTS.
I'M A SWIMMER. A MARTIAL ARTIST. A DANCER...
INDIA INCLUSION SUMMIT

...A HUSBAND AND A FATHER.
I MET MY WIFE, LAKSHMI, DURING AN EVENT AT A SCHOOL WHERE SHE WAS A TEACHER. WITHIN A FEW DAYS OF TALKING, WE KNEW WE WANTED TO SPEND THE REST OF OUR LIVES TOGETHER. WE SOON GOT MARRIED WITH BLESSINGS FROM BOTH OUR FAMILIES, AND WE NOW HAVE A WONDERFUL DAUGHTER, PRASHASTI, WHO JUST TURNED ONE.
MY WIFE HAS BEEN MY PILLAR OF STRENGTH. SHE TAUGHT ME TO KEEP MY FACE TO THE SUN DURING THE PANDEMIC WHEN ALL THE SWIMMING AND DANCING EVENTS – MY ONLY SOURCE OF INCOME – WERE CANCELLED.
INDIA INCLUSIO SUMMIT
THIS IS JUST A TEMPORARY PHASE, VISHWA. WE'LL SAIL THROUGH THIS TOGETHER. DON'T BE DISHEARTENED. THINK OF WHY YOU BEGAN DOING ALL THESE!
AH, YES. THE 'WHY'.
I CHOSE TO BE INVOLVED IN THESE ACTIVITIES BECAUSE I HAD ALL THE TIME IN THE WORLD. I WANTED TO COME OUT OF MY LETHARGIC LIFESTYLE.
NOW, I CONTINUE TO DO ALL THIS BECAUSE...

...WELL, BECAUSE I CAN!
NOT JUST THESE. I HAVE -
- RUN MARATHONS,
12
- COMPETED IN SEA SWIMMING EVENTS, WHICH, BY THE WAY, WAS A LOT MORE CHALLENGING THAN POOL SWIMMING.
- BEEN ON A MICRO FLIGHT,
- SCUBA-DIVED IN GOA,
AND EVEN ACTED IN A MOVIE!
Arabbie

I DON'T LET MY DISABLITY DECIDE WHAT I CAN OR CANNOT DO.
I DO THE THINGS THAT CHALLENGE ME, AND BRING ME JOY.
I CONSIDER MYSELF VERY FORTUNATE TO HAVE HAD ALL THESE EXPERIENCES.
WHEREVER I WENT, I FOUND IMMENSE SUPPORT. MY COACHES AND TRAINERS TAUGHT ME FOR FREE.
YES, I DO FACE REJECTION MORE OFTEN THAN ACCEPTANCE.
BUT, INSTEAD OF FIGHTING, I'VE LEARNT TO TAKE IT IN MY STRIDE.
I'VE COME TO REALIZE THAT PEOPLE SOMETIMES BEHAVE DIFFERENTLY BECAUSE THEY DON'T HAVE MUCH EXPOSURE TO SUCH MATTERS OR COME ACROSS DISABLED PEOPLE ON AN EVERYDAY BASIS.
THEIR NATURAL REACTION IS MOSTLY SYMPATHY.

SYMPATHY IS NOT WHAT WE WANT. WE JUST WANT OPPORTUNITIES. A HELPING HAND.
EVERY HUMAN NEEDS THE SUPPORT OF ANOTHER PERSON.
DISABLED PEOPLE NEED A LITTLE BIT MORE, THAT'S ALL.
I DON'T KNOW HOW MUCH SUPPORT OTHER DISABLED PEOPLE HAVE. BUT I HAVE ALWAYS HAD THE ENCOURAGEMENT OF MY FAMILY, MY FRIENDS WHO'VE BEEN WITH ME SINCE CLASS NINE, AND ALL MY WELL-WISHERS AT EVERY STAGE.
AND I'M CONFIDENT THAT I'LL MEET MANY SUCH PEOPLE IN MY LIFE - THAT'S WHAT I BELIEVE IN.
IT IS THIS BELIEF THAT MOTIVATES ME TO NOT LOSE HOPE.
IT IS THIS BELIEF THAT INSPIRES ME TO TAKE ON NEW CHALLENGES AND GIVE MY BEST.
BECAUSE WHAT CHOICE DO I HAVE OTHER THAN TO HAVE FAITH.

MY NAME IS VISHWAS.
AND I'M A BELIEVER.

Vishwas K.S. is an international para-swimming champion, motivational speaker, dancer and martial artist. He has represented India in prestigious para-swimming competitions and has secured numerous medals. In 2016, he won two silver and one bronze at the Speedo Can Am Para-Swimming Championships held in Ottawa, Canada. He followed this successful streak by landing another bronze at the IDM Berlin Para Swimming German Open in 2017 and 2018. At the National Para Swimming Competition in Udaipur, he won a gold and two silver. He then took the count higher by winning five gold medals at the Indian Open Swimming Competition, Bengaluru, in 2018.

Vishwas has been conferred several prestigious state, national and international awards – most notably the Special Golden Achiever Award by AUGP, US; National Role Model Award by the former vice president of India (2018); Kempegowda Award; the Vishweshwariah Ratna Award; and the Shoorveer Award by Ample Missiion, Mumbai. He hopes to live a life of dignity, self-reliance, and financial independence. It is his deep desire to initiate public dialogue around disability and bring substantial change in the world.

He currently lives in Bengaluru with his wife, Lakshmi, and his daughter, Prashasti. The royalties from the sale of this book will go to his family.

(Email: vishwasks303@gmail.com; Instagram: @vishwasksvishu; Mobile: +91 9972530303)

V.R. Ferose is a software executive based in Silicon Valley and is an author, columnist and inclusion evangelist. He is the founder of India Inclusion Foundation, a Bengaluru-based non-profit organization that aims to bring acceptance and inclusion for the disabled to the forefront. Ferose was selected as a Young Global Leader by the World Economic Forum in 2012. He was featured in 'India's 40 under 40' list in 2014 and was recognized with the AUCD award by US Senator Tom Harkin for his path-breaking initiative 'Autism at Work' at SAP. Simultaneously, he has co-authored bestsellers such as *Gifted: Inspiring Stories of People with Disabilities* (2014) and *The Invisible Majority* (2021). He writes the biweekly column FLYLEAF for *New Indian Express*. He lives in Cupertino with his wife, Deepali, and son, Vivaan.

(Website: www.ferosevr.com; Email: ferosevr2015@gmail.com; Twitter: @VRFerose)

Sriram Jagannathan is a writer, illustrator and designer from Chennai. He is a consultant and mentor in the User Experience space for digital products and helps organizations by advocating for design thinking to C-suite players. His experience in design spans multiple spheres – fashion, textile design, web-based courseware, animation branding, sportswear and graphic novels. The threads that connect his many ventures are creativity and storytelling, his first love. He is also a firm believer in the power of art and design to transform how we experience the world. Sriram is the author of two graphic novels: *Mai*, published by Notion Press in 2018, and *Grit: The Major Story*, published by Hachette India in 2019. This is his third book.

(Email: sriramjag@gmail.com; Instagram: @sriramjag)